the
ORIGINAL GREEN
[UNLOCKING *the* MYSTERY *of* TRUE SUSTAINABILITY]

STEPHEN A. MOUZON

Foreword by
ROBERT F. KENNEDY, JR.

THE GUILD FOUNDATION PRESS
Miami

in association with
THE INSTITUTE OF CLASSICAL ARCHITECTURE AND CLASSICAL AMERICA

ISBN 1-931871-11-6

10 9 8 7 6 5 4 3 2 1

DESIGN, PHOTOGRAPHY, *and* DRAWINGS

Stephen A. Mouzon
This book was set using Bembo Std and Futura Std fonts.

PRINTING

3 Dimension Graphics, Inc.
8031 NW 14th Street
Doral, Florida 33126

DISTRIBUTION

The Guild Foundation Press
1253 Washington Avenue, Suite 222
Miami Beach, Florida 33139
www.guildfoundation.org

This book owes significant debts to a large number of other people and to many publications. The historical facts upon which this book are based are commonly available in many sources, but were verified in the publications listed in the Bibliography and the websites listed in the Links section, both located in the Resources chapter at the end of this book.

CREDITS

This book would not have been possible without the love, support, and patience of my wife and partner, Wanda Mouzon or my most excellent editor, Nancy Bruning. Thanks also to all my clients who have allowed me to test these ideas, and to their craftsmen who built from them. Credit is also due to the many colleagues who refined these ideas on listservs, Original Green and Useful Stuff blog comments, on Facebook, and in person, and who have long urged me to put these Original Green ideas into print.

GUILD FOUNDATION

NEW URBAN GUILD

FOREWORD

In 1996, my family was enjoying a Cape Cod vacation when a deluge inundated our Mt. Kisco, New York, home, a sprawling clapboard 1920 structure astride an 1870 stone foundation, all treacherously encased in 1950's era aluminum siding. Standing water from the flood caused a black mold bloom that, thriving in the moisture trapped inside by the building's metallic skin, colonized the upper stories like a Petri dish, sickening our children and frustrating every effort at removal.

Even as a nature lover, I balked as fecund spores painted the walls and ceilings an ominous grey before subsiding into my bedroom in a fine mist. We fought a two year losing battle against the creeping fungus. Finally, in 2005, after unsuccessfully attempting a gut renovation, we realized the only solution was to raze and rebuild.

Although sad about losing our century-old family home, I was excited by the prospect of building a green house. I figured it was about time I started walking the walk in my own home. I felt well-equipped to handle the task. My wife, Mary Richardson, had been a green designer and architect for over two decades. Now, Mary was anxious to turn her talents to greening her own crib. We began with several criteria. We wanted the house to be beautiful, practical, comfortable and above all lovable. We also wanted to stay on a disciplined budget. People who live in green houses save money by consuming less energy and less water than standard homes and suffering fewer days of missed work from illnesses. Green homes are more durable than conventional structures and require fewer repairs. Mary is a militant opponent of our throw-away culture. She designed the structure around traditional brick jack-arches in our home which will provide structural integrity for a millennium, in contrast to conventional steel beams which rust out in 50 years.

Mary made sure that after its demolition, the old house was 100% recycled. Another obstacle was to minimize the use of virgin materials in our construction. She carefully selected toxin-free building materials to help combat indoor air pollution. Her designs rely on natural ventilation, as well as use of mechanical ventilation systems to filter and bring fresh air inside and vent stale air outside to keep our family breathing easy. She installed super efficient plumbing and bathing fixtures, drought-tolerant landscaping, and a water-conserving irrigation system to dramatically reduce water use in our home. Mary designed a classically elegant Georgian brick structure with large, airy and well-lit rooms and hallways that blends perfectly with the landscape and character of our community. Our home is tightly insulated, with super efficient lighting and appliances, and powered by geothermal and solar panels. We used efficient appliances and fiber optic, low voltage, high efficiency LED light bulbs. Through design efficiencies and energy-saving lighting and appliances, our green home will use about half the energy of a comparable standard home.

Green is the new red, white and blue. We are proud to be participating in the "new energy" economy, which will soon free our country from her deadly addiction to foreign oil and toxic coal. Energy self-sufficiency is a patriotic duty for every American. It will improve our national security and preserve us from oil wars and demeaning entanglements with foreign dictators who despise democracy. Moreover, a distributed power system owned by tens of millions of American homeowners is not only more democratic than a power system controlled by a few wealthy plutocrats - it is more reliable, more resilient and far less vulnerable to attack by our enemies.

Coal is just as bad for America as oil. Whatever the slick campaign financed by the powerful coal barons might claim, coal is neither cheap nor clean. Ozone and particulates from coal plants kill tens of thousands of Americans each year and cause widespread illnesses and disease. Acid rain from coal stacks has destroyed millions of acres of valuable forests. Coal industry strip mines have already destroyed 500 mountains in Appalachia, buried 2,000 miles of rivers and streams and will soon have flattened an area the size of Delaware. Finally, coal, which supplies 46 percent of our electric power, is the most prolific source of America's greenhouse gases which threaten civilization and the lives and livelihoods of millions around the globe.

America is blessed with abundant renewable energy resources—wind, solar, tidal, geothermal and biomass—but our biggest potential for low cost megawatts will come from the energy savings—or "negawatts"—we get from exploiting all the hidden opportunities for efficiency in our built environment. I hope that you learn more from our family's experience and find a way to incorporate some of these techniques into your home. By greening your own crib you can help our country to solve our most urgent national problems—global warming, national security, our staggering debt, and a stagnant economy. By kicking its carbon addiction, America will increase its national wealth and generate millions of jobs that can't be outsourced. We will create a decentralized and highly distributable and democratic grid. We will cut annual trade and budget deficits by hundreds of billions and improve public health and farm production. And for the first time in half a century we will live free from Middle Eastern wars and entanglements with petty tyrants who damage our international prestige and our historical reputation as an exemplary nation.

ROBERT F. KENNEDY, JR.

CONTENTS

CHIEF AMONGST *the* GIANTS *on* WHOSE SHOULDERS THIS BOOK STANDS:

His Royal Highness the Prince of Wales is in so many ways a clear portrait of what a world leader should look like. His vision of a sustainable world filled with sustainable places often stands cross-current to powerful institutions, but the courage exhibited in laying the truth against orthodoxy should be an inspiration to us all.

Léon Krier is the architect and theorist that first turned the paths of many of my colleagues as well as my own out of the mainstream and on to a better way. His incisive cartoons skewer modern-day conventional thinking like none other of our age, and his drawings' clarity in laying out the principles of a better place remain essential to us all.

Christopher Alexander developed the idea that a language of patterns shared by many is required to create a living place. This pattern language structure is essential to many principles of the Original Green. Without these ideas framing a timeless way of building, it is doubtful that the mysteries laid out in this book would ever have been unlocked.

Andrés Duany co-founded the New Urbanism and continues to be its most influential voice. His uncanny articulation the vague sense of unease spawned by sprawl has turned countless people away from this most unsustainable way of making places. But more personally, his invitation to move to Miami several years ago completely changed my career.

Elizabeth Plater-Zyberk also co-founded the New Urbanism, and brings together its disparate constituents like none other. She spearheads change in many arenas, from running the mammoth Miami21 rezoning to serving as Dean of the School of Architecture at the University of Miami, where she took me under her wing and began to teach me how to teach.

Nathan Norris, an attorney by trade but an urbanist by heart, began cross-examining my unpolished ideas a decade ago. Without Nathan, this book would not exist. He has also opened the towns and neighborhoods where he has worked to my experiments, enabling many of these ideas to stand in the confidence of things that have been proven.

INTRODUCTION

The Original Green is the sustainability all our ancestors knew by heart. Originally (before the Thermostat Age) they had no choice but to build green, otherwise people would not survive very long. The Original Green aggregates and distributes the wisdom of sustainability through the operating system of living traditions, because that which can reproduce and live sustainably is green; that which is incapable of doing so is not green. This is the standard of life. Life is that process which creates all things green.

The Original Green produces sustainable places in which it is meaningful to build sustainable buildings, with sustainability that is common-sense and plain-spoken, meaning "keeping things going in a healthy way long into an uncertain future." Sustainable places are nourishable, accessible, serviceable, and securable. Serviceable places, for example, are those where you can get all your daily services within walking distance, and where you can choose to make a living where you're living if you want to. Sustainable buildings are lovable, durable, flexible, and frugal. They're lovable, for example, because if a building can't be loved, it won't last.

Unfortunately, the living traditions that were the operating systems of the Original Green faltered and then died in regions around the world over a few decades as industrialization reached its high point in each of those regions, and with their

deaths, the Original Green faded into our current unsustainable ways of life. Now, the question is: how do we establish new living traditions, so that we can once again achieve true sustainability? We can't just go back to the 15th century because we're 21st century people. So how do we do it? This is the great mystery that this book hopes to begin to unlock. We'll need to be open-minded and creative in order to find the keys.

How This Book *is* Arranged

This book has four parts. *Part One ~ What's the Problem?* is where we will take a look at the top ten things we're doing right now to be green that can't get the job done... things like Gizmo Green, which is the supposition that better equipment and some bamboo for good measure can make us green. While important, these measures are only a small part of true sustainability. In *Part Two ~ What Can We Do?* we'll examine the true breadth of what it takes to really be green, focusing on the top ten principles that should support true sustainability. These principles guide the construction of Original Green places and buildings.

The four foundations of sustainable places and the four foundations of sustainable buildings are laid out in detail in

Part Three ~ What's the Plan? These foundations are things that, if fully implemented, will require your entire community. But it all gets personal in *Part Four ~ What Can I Do?* There, I detail the top ten things that each of us can do individually to be green... beginning today! Finally, I've included a *Resources* section at the end of the book which I hope you'll find helpful.

HOW IT WORKS

We'll look at all these things in detail later, but let's start with a surprising story of one way the ideas in this book might operate: I was a team member on a design charrette for the Rose Town neighborhood in Kingston, Jamaica in the autumn of 2008 sponsored by the Prince's Foundation for the Built Environment. Prince Charles had visited Rose Town several years earlier, and was so moved by the plight of its residents that he adopted its improvement as one of his causes. Because I've written architectural codes for years, and because I had recently completed A Living Tradition [Architecture of the Bahamas] (where many conditions are similar)

my assigned role on the charrette team was to write the code that would guide future construction in Rose Town.

The Rose Town neighborhood has become desperately poor over the past several decades. The luckiest residents live in crumbling remains of the old homes. Less fortunate neighbors live in tin shacks they've built for themselves with scavenged materials. Others have only a ramshackle tin fence around a spot of land, and sleep out on the ground, with no roof over their heads. If you want electricity in Rose Town, you attach wires to coat hanger hooks and throw them up over the powerlines overhead. There are reportedly six working toilets in the entire neighborhood, but they flush only if you bring in bottles of water because there's no water service.

I've worked in Rose Town before as part of the Prince's ongoing efforts there, but on the first day of the charrette the design team was walking through the neighborhood and I was struck by something I hadn't noticed before: Walls lining the streets are often painted with what I call proverbs. Sometimes they're proverbs from the Bible, but often, they're simply instructions on how to live better, such as the proverb shown in this image. They aren't graffiti scrawled hurriedly on the walls with spray cans, as you can see. Rather, they're pains-

takingly painted; the more elaborate ones might take a day or two to complete. Because of my previous Rose Town experience, there was never any doubt in my mind that a normal code book (which is normally 200-300 pages long) would never work because it would be too expensive, so I was looking for alternatives. It occurred to me during that first walk that I might be able to write a code using proverbs about how to build better, so that the document could be very short.

The finished code contained items like these: "Build your house on higher ground so that the floods do not make you homeless." "Raise the floor of your house at least half your height above the ground because even the higher ground will flood in the worst of storms." "Build your ceilings high, up to twice your height or more, so that the hot air can rise, keeping you cooler."

A sample page from the code:

2 • DOORS & WINDOWS

WINDOW SHUTTERS

Protect your windows with solid board shutters, so that you can quickly shut the shutters to protect your home when the storm is on its way.

COOL BREEZE

Build at least one window on each end of your house that is either under a tree or under a verandah so you can leave these windows open and pull cool air into your home.

The code was only ten pages long, and most of the space on each page was taken up with the little square drawing for each item. But on the day before the charrette ended, I began to have a growing sense of unease about the code. I grew up in the Deep South; when I was a child in the 1960s, some people were still using outhouses. I remember finding the Sears Catalog in some of those outhouses being repurposed because the

The first proverb, painted on a rainy day on the street wall of
the library, which just 6 months before, had been a deserted
building, but was renovated by the Prince's Foundation.

catalog was free and toilet paper wasn't. Recalling this, it became clear that the ten pages of my code would likely meet the same fate in very short order in Rose Town. But then it occurred to me: why not do what the people do? Why not paint the proverbs on the walls of the streets?

So on the last day of the charrette, one of our team members took the last item in the code and painted it on the wall just outside the neighborhood library we were using for our charrette studio. Here's what it says: "Plant your yard with things you can eat, for why should your yard lay fallow while you spend more of your money at the grocery store?" She finished painting it just before the final presentation. We hope to have the others painted on walls around Rose Town at some point in the not-too-distant future.

The crowd of attendees were still milling around talking after the presentation when a young Kingston architect tugged my arm and said "Steve, you've gotta see this!" "What is it," I asked as I turned toward him. "Come and see." So we made our way to the front of the building through the crowd.

As we stepped out the door into the night air, I could hear the voices of children singing. I hurried to the street and found these children, standing before the proverb on the wall. They were taking these simple words that were never meant to have rhythm or rhyme, and they were turning them into a song!

We can't make this happen. We can only set the stage for something like this to happen. But I now have high hopes this completely unexpected Kingston evening may have unlocked a part of the mystery of sustainability by showing a way for people to make new traditions their own.

Part One
What's *the* Problem?

The Top 10 Problems with Our Current Green Efforts

The policies we are employing now to achieve sustainability are not winning strategies. They can help a larger strategy win, but they, by themselves, cannot do the job because they focus only on small parts of the problem of living sustainably today.

That is *really* bad news because for the first time in human history, we're faced with a problem so important that nearly every industrialized nation says that they're committed (to varying degrees) to solving it. And every major corporation says they're working on it, too. The stakes exceed anything humanity has ever seen. Few of the major long-term energy, resource, or ecological trends that currently exist can be sustained without catastrophic consequences, as we'll see later.

Much has been written recently about the implications of peak oil, the environment, and now the economic meltdown that became global while this book was being written. I won't attempt to repeat the cases that others have very capably made. Rather, this book aims to chart a way through the menaces we're facing... so please keep reading, because it turns much more hopeful after this first chapter. Here's a quick look at the top ten problems:

10 *the* Absence *of* Plain-Spoken Sustainability is a problem throughout nearly all current discussions on the issue. The word "sustainability" ought to mean "keeping things going in a healthy way long into an uncertain future." Sadly, the meaning of the word today is something more like "the newest buzz-word for selling my products."

9 *the* Danger *of* Wishes is found in the growing number of sustainability targets out there that can best be characterized as wishes that other people would solve sustainability.

8 *the* Dilemma *of* Global Warming is the fact that global warming has become a highly politicized

idea in the last couple decades. This means that the idea is very divisive at a time when we need everyone working together.

7 *the* Fate *of* "Ought-To" is that we don't usually do the things we ought to do. Things that get done are the things we want to do or the things we have to do.

6 *the* Problem *of* Growth runs counter to common thought. For a century, the primary measure of economic health has been growth. Places want to grow, businesses want to grow, etc. But what happens when we run out of room to grow, and what precious things do we lose along the way?

5 *the* Trouble *with* Consumption. We all have been trained to see ourselves as consumers, but the end result of consuming is a lot of garbage and dwindling resources. Consider the benefits of a Conserving Economy rather than a Consuming Economy.

4 *the* Achilles Heel *of* Architecture is the assertion that if you want to be significant, you must be unique. But uniqueness is the enemy of sustainability in a number of ways.

3 *the* Carbon Focus is the illusion that if we reduce the carbon dioxide output of our buildings, everything will be fine. This illusion is quite strong right now, but we'll see how rushing down this path alone cannot be a winning strategy.

2 *the* Supply-Side Focus is the error of focusing on changing the things we buy, rather than changing the things we do. In other words, we're asking our suppliers to change, but we're not really asking ourselves to change.

1 *the* Problem *of the* Two *and a* Half Billion People is the largest of all. Until recently, the lifestyle of the American middle class was the world's biggest ecological problem, but there

are now two and a half billion people around the world who are in the process of adopting our lifestyle, so multiply by nine.

Now, let's take a look at the details of these 10 problems...

10 ~ *the* ABSENCE *of* PLAIN-SPOKEN SUSTAINABILITY

"Sustainability" is one of the most misused terms on the planet today... and that's dangerous. It seems that it can mean almost anything, but that really means that it means nothing. So how can we reach a meaningless goal?

To the thousands of companies who are currently working on proving that their products are the most sustainable things you could buy, sustainability is not much more than marketing fluff. The problem is, most companies aren't changing their products to be greener; they're just changing their sales pitches so they can tell you how green they already are. This is a practice known as "greenwashing," which is a huge disservice to us all.

How *to* Fix It

Sustainability ought to have a strong meaning, and in this book, it does. Whenever you read the word here, you can count on it having this common-sense, plain-spoken definition: "keeping things going in a healthy way long into an uncertain future" because if it doesn't last, it's not sustainable.

9 ~ *the* Danger *of* Wishes

Sustainability targets are predestined for failure. And let's be clear: I am fully in support of the two programs that will be described here. But all target programs have a core problem which we'll get to in a moment. But first, let's look at a couple:

I have great admiration for Ed Mazria, who has single-handedly taken a great idea and pushed it tirelessly until it has

gotten onto many people's radar screens across the US and abroad. Ed has become the model, in many ways, of what I am attempting to do with the Original Green: one person (in the beginning) setting out to make a difference starting with nothing but a great idea, but resulting in many people joining the cause.

Ed's great idea is an initiative that he calls Architecture 2030; it's a call for all new

buildings to be carbon-neutral by 2030. Check out his site (www.architecture2030.org) for details.

The British government has issued an even bigger challenge, calling for all buildings in the UK to be carbon-neutral starting in 2016. Go to www.communities.gov.uk/planningandbuilding/theenvironment for details. Other countries are adopting carbon targets; a web search returns a growing list.

So what's the problem? Targets that may be characterized as "you should do this..." simply are not as compelling as those that begin as "I will do this..." "You should do this..." targets are a special kind of wishful thinking: they are the things you wish someone else would do, rather than the things you're willing to commit to yourself. Even when wishful thinking targets carry the force of law, such as the British 2016 target, they are susceptible to being missed. What will the government do if the British construction industry hasn't figured out how to be carbon-neutral by 2016 in a manner that most citizens can afford? Will office-holders have the guts to shut down the entire construction industry until they figure it out?

How Can Targets Work?

Targets are not without merit. Probably the most notable success was President Kennedy's call for putting man on the moon. Without it, Apollo 11 would never have occurred. But we should not be lulled into thinking that everything's okay just because we have carbon targets. The thing that makes targets work is when leaders with great resolve say "*I* will do this..." or better yet, when all of us commit to doing so.

The disappearance of snow cover is one piece of evidence that doesn't require complicated scientific explanations because we can see it with our own eyes.

8 ~ *the* DILEMMA *of* GLOBAL WARMING

This is the only part of this book that will be explicitly about politics... I promise. Anyone who is a serious advocate for sustainability in the US needs to face up to the fact that we have a big problem.

Yale University's School of Forestry and Environmental Studies found in July 2007 that "... a large majority of the American public is personally convinced that global warming is happening (71%). Surprisingly, however, only 48 percent believe that there is consensus among the scientific community, while 40 percent of Americans still believe there is a lot of disagreement among scientists over whether global warming is occurring." I can understand that, to a degree, if this were 1990 rather than 2010. I am old enough to remember the debate in the 1970s as to whether we were going to have global warming or global cooling. That debate made me a skeptic of global warming for years. I was finally convinced, however, by the glacier photos. Remember Hemingway's *The Snows of Kilimanjaro*? Well, if you look at photos of Mount Kilimanjaro taken in Hemingway's day versus photos taken today (at the same time of the year) the difference is shocking... as are images of numerous glaciers around the world. I generally do not argue with evidence my eyes can clearly see.

Here's another bit of evidence I have seen with my own eyes, and which stunningly confirmed the glacier photos: I was in Europe in 2003, and on our return flight just after the 4th of July, the pilot said "If you can, move to the right side of the plane, because you're about to see something you may never see again. We are on a flight path further North than normal, and we're about to fly past Greenland. This is probably the only time you will ever see Greenland."

I moved to the right side, of course, and will forever regret that I left my camera packed away in the overhead bins. The gorgeous snowy mountains billowed away to the horizon. It was a stunning sight forever to be imprinted on my mind.

This year, I was in Europe again, except it was a month earlier in the year; I was returning in early June. I grew increasingly more excited as it became apparent that we were on the same flight path over Greenland on which we had been five years earlier. Anxiously, I retrieved my camera this time, and gripped it, unwilling to miss such a beautiful sight again.

But as we crossed over the coast, my anticipation turned to shock and disbelief. The landscape that had been such a beautiful wonderland just five years before melted away before my eyes. Where billowy mountains of snow had stretched endlessly on the previous flight, I now saw only rocky slopes, and the small bits of remaining snow and ice slipping off them into the sea. My disbelief was so great that my camera hung there useless... I didn't even think to shoot what I was seeing.

As for me, nobody will ever again convince me that global warming is not happening, because I have seen it with my own eyes. It is not some hypothetical possibility, but rather, it is something which I have witnessed.

But there is a problem with global warming. Hundreds of millions of Americans were not on the plane with me that day (or on the day several years earlier when I finally had to confront the glacier photos and give up my long-held skepticism,) and if the

Yale study is to be believed, there are still tens of millions of Americans who have serious misgivings about the truth of global warming, and about its origins.

The major culprit in this situation is politics. It has not always been that way. Strangely (from today's point of view,) Richard Nixon (a Republican) presided over the creation of the Environmental Protection Agency. And on the first Earth Day just a few months earlier, it seemed that there was wide agreement among Americans of all political stripes that our natural environment was in critical condition.

It was not long, however, until the bipartisanship dissolved into polarization over the environment. It does not matter who fired the first shots; Republicans say it was Carter, while Democrats say it was Reagan. For the purposes of this book, it's immaterial. Here's why:

Democrats clearly are identified today as protectors of the environment, while Republicans are tagged as the desecrators. There are many reasons for this; some of them well-earned, and some of them pure political posturing (on both sides.)

How *to* Fix It

Here is this book's most important political message: *Get over it!!!*

[21]

If you're a Republican, *get over it!* An overwhelming majority of scientists agree global warming is real, but our future is bigger than any lost debate. We need your help... *today!*

If you're a Democrat, *get over it!* So you won the debate.... what's more important now... to spend your time rubbing your opponents' collective noses in it, or to spend your time in actually *doing* something about global warming?

Put another way... *We need all hands on deck... now!!!* If we plan to act like Americans and buckle down and get the job done, then the last thing we need is for one side to gloat, or for the other side to leave the table. So *Get Over It... NOW!!!* Let's all pitch in and do the American thing and get the job done! Anything less is unacceptable. *(One more thing: the rest of the book applies regardless of your stand on global warming.)*

7 ~ *the* FATE *of* "OUGHT-TO"

Okay, I'll take a deep breath while you Google "sustainability." It won't take you very long to find lengthy lists of things we ought to do. These lists are all but useless. Why is this?

Real sustainability, as we'll see later on, is something that can only be accomplished when pretty much everyone makes changes. "You ought to…" doesn't get the job done.

Sustainability is not something that the manufacturers, government, trade organizations, or specialists will do for us; it's something that begins with things we do for ourselves. The others can help, but they cannot do it for us, because the job is simply too immense. There are three major reasons people make big changes: "have to," "ought to," or "want to."

[23]

HAVE-TO

"Have to" is the reason that means there isn't any other choice. During the summer of 2008 when gas briefly spiked to $5/gallon in most parts of the US, many people realized that they simply couldn't afford to live where they were living. Had gas stayed that high, they would have been forced to make hard choices that would have been very traumatic for most of them. Choices that involved moving somewhere less desirable and less affordable to be near their work, or getting an undesirable job near home. So "have to" works, but it's normally quite painful.

OUGHT-TO

The "ought to" reason is used to frame most of the sustainability solutions in-tended for the population at large. You ought to recycle. You ought to drive less. You ought to adjust your ther-mostat. Unfortunately, people very seldom do what they ought to do. "Ought to" sounds like a good reason for *someone else* to do something, but not a good reason for *me* to do something. As a result, "ought to" simply doesn't work with most people. In other words, even though

Have-To, Ought-To, or Want-To:
Is there any doubt which is the
best driver of human behavior?

we can't achieve sustainability without everyone doing things differently, the main tool that is currently being used to persuade people ("you ought to") simply doesn't work on enough people to make a real difference. It may make us feel better to compile lists of things people ought to do, but this is not a winning strategy for real results; it is doomed to fail. If you doubt this, check your New Year's resolutions in February.

WANT-TO

"Want to" is often ignored in sustainability discussions. People want to do something because they love to do it or because they believe it will benefit them in some way. Their emotion or their intellect is telling them to do it. Wanting to is highly effective because it's positive. Rather than avoiding pain like you do with a "have to" reason, you're doing something because of the pleasure or benefit it brings. We'll see later how "want to" reasons are the foundations of the living tradition, which is the operating system of the only proven delivery system for real sustainability: the Original Green.

6 ~ *the* PROBLEM *of* GROWTH

The American idea of growth is seriously screwed up in such a way that it prevents us from building green places. Every Chamber of Commerce in the US has economic growth as one of its top priorities. Most cities aspired to grow, and grow they did, especially after World War II. Our economic health is measured by a growing Gross Domestic Product. But there is a problem: Can we really continue growing forever?

The image on the opposite page shows what will happen to Florida if growth continues along current trends. In 50 years, you can see that with the exception of the Lake Okeechobee

area and patches of park land, the peninsula will pretty much be one enormous city. What then? A half-century is a short period in the time scale of urbanism, where cities can live for two thousand years or more. Add another hundred years to the Florida timeline and it's clear that there will be no farmland remaining anywhere in the state. And then what?

Somehow, we must come to grips with the idea that growth, as good as it may sound, and as enticing as it may be, simply is not sustainable. We cannot grow larger forever. I realize that this may be shocking to you; it was shocking to me when I first tried to get my mind around the idea. But if we are serious about sustainability, then we must figure out how to keep things going for a long time. And a path that has us running

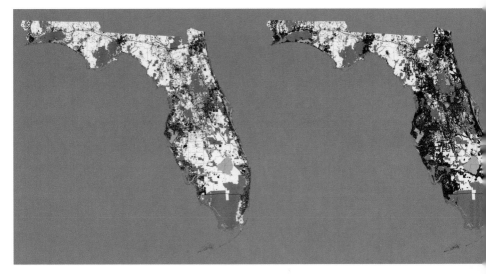

Florida today and in 50 years, from the Florida 2060 report sponsored by 1000 Friends of Florida.

out of things (including land) in the foreseeable future isn't going to allow us to keep things going. In other words, that course of action, by definition, is not sustainable.

If growing forever is not sustainable, what is? We will see later in this book that nature provides many excellent models. Consider nature's growth model: People are conceived as a single cell and grow in the womb until birth. We then grow to our final height at a fairly early age; often between 16 and 20 years old. From that point forward, our physical size remains (hopefully) about the same for the rest of our lives. But we can grow in many other ways: We can grow wiser, we can grow more talented, we can grow more athletic, we can grow more cultured, or more able in many other ways as we mature.

If this is nature's way of growth, why should this not be cities' way of growth as well? What if cities were to decide that "we're not going to get any larger on the land, but we will get better; we will get stronger; we will become more cultured; we will become wiser." The population could still grow, of course, but the city could accommodate that through growing more compact rather than sprawling. This is nothing new; for millennia, cities grew by growing more compact rather than growing out; they just haven't done it so much recently.

A few American cities are already trying crude versions of this idea. Portland's Urban Growth Boundary is the most famous. But the problem with Portland is that while it has been growing more compact, the growth inside the Urban Growth Boundary is of no higher quality than the recent sprawling growth in any other American city; it is merely denser. So for nature's way of growth to really work for cities, the quality of

The little girl has lots of growing yet to do. The old man quit growing taller many years ago, but is clearly still growing in other ways.

life must also increase, not just the density. So let's go ahead and face up to the fact that we cannot grow larger forever. This is the failed policy of sprawl; it is fundamentally unsustainable. But we can grow better without limits. It is nature's way to grow; why should it not be ours?

5 ~ *the* TROUBLE *with* CONSUMPTION

We know we are all consumers, and we don't give it a second thought... but we should, because the Consuming Economy is unsustainable. The trouble with consumption is related to the problem of growth: our economic health is measured by growth of the economy, and the machine that drives that growth is consumption.

Our ancestors would likely have been horrified by the consumption paradigm. Probably half of the adages of their times had something to do with conserving instead of consuming: "Waste not, want not." "A penny saved is a penny earned." "A stitch in time saves nine." "An ounce of prevention is worth a pound of cure," etc. And their stories of frugality and conservation that have filtered down to our day are nearly endless. Conservation allowed them to keep things going for a really long time: it allowed them to live in a sustainable fashion.

Consumption, on the other hand, requires us to continue extracting things from the earth, fabricating them into useful things, then discarding those things when they have lost

their usefulness to us, or when we have lost interest in them. Consumption is the path from resources to garbage. A nation of consumers produces a nation full of garbage. The tallest mountain within hundreds of miles of my home in South Beach is a trash heap.

So what's the alternative? What would an economy look like based primarily on conservation rather than consumption and how would it improve our quality of life and our sustainability? Let's try to imagine:

the Conserving Economy: Manufacturing

Some segments would clearly be smaller. If we built things to last rather than to be thrown away, the business of building appliances, cars, and even buildings with unwritten expiration dates would be much smaller.

Planned obsolescence is a scheme invented by industry to make things designed to wear out after limited life so that you have to keep buying more stuff from the manufacturer. This idea has only been around since approximately 1925, which is a significant date discussed in detail later in this book, and which I believe is the beginning of the Great Decline.

Before planned obsolescence, things were treasured because they lasted. Furniture that was well-built became family heirlooms, handed down for generations. Tools were used for an entire career, and then handed down to the next generation who treasured them as they worked with them, too. As a matter of fact, the value of a tool or furnishing derived in large part from its ability to endure. So a Conserving Economy would make a lot less stuff, because the stuff it made would last a lot longer. Wouldn't that cost American jobs? News flash:

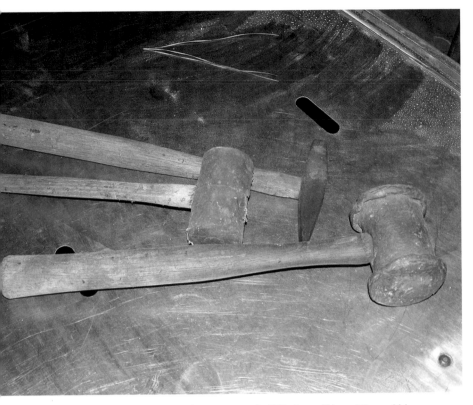

A repair shop is extremely difficult to offshore. We would be buying fewer things from overseas if we were insisting that those things were made to last.

Most manufacturing jobs departed from American shores a decade or two ago.

the CONSERVING ECONOMY: MAINTENANCE & REPAIR

There are other implications, as you might guess. If things were built to last, then they would occasionally need help along the way in the form of maintenance and repair. But maintenance and repair jobs are full of problems for big business. Whereas the manufacturing of widgets can be done in huge quantity with a manageable and fairly predictable flow of materials and labor, maintenance and repair jobs happen one at a time... or maybe ten at a time. You really can't predict them that well.

And whereas manufacturing can be done anywhere and the products shipped globally (for now,) maintenance and repair jobs are much more commonly done near where the product is used. Who do you know that actually likes to ship something off to have it repaired? And people don't care how long it took to make a product, but they care very much how long it takes to fix it.

As a result, maintenance and repair jobs are harder to outsource, and much harder to offshore. And because these jobs don't fit the big business paradigm very well, they are left to small businesses most of the time. So what's wrong with enhancing a sector that supports small business and that is resistant to offshoring?

the Conserving Economy: Life-Cycle Cost

Things that last longer clearly cost more, but if you divide that cost over the

*The Pantheon and the plaza it helps create are still being
enjoyed by Romans (and many others) nearly 2,000 years
after its construction.*

much-expanded lifespan of the thing, then your cost per
year is much less. Consider "millennium buildings": you may
spend 50% more for a building that will last 1,000 years instead of lasting 100 years. But the cost per year of the 1,000-
year building is only 15% of the cost per year of the 100-year
building. And most buildings built today aren't even meant to

last 100 years! Because developers don't care about anything this long-term, calls for lower life-cycle costs must come from the public; it must become part of the ethos of our culture again, as it once was.

the CONSERVING ECONOMY: QUALITY OF LIFE

The transition from a Consuming Economy to a Conserving Economy will be expensive at first, but that should come as no surprise since the recovery from almost any mistake is costly at some point along the recovery path. But once the recovery has taken place, then our cost per year of maintaining our quality of life will be substantially less.

Why "quality of life" rather than "standard of living"? Because the "standard of living" yardstick is what you use to measure the vigor of a Consuming Economy. Standard of living is the measure of how many things we have, and how big they are. It's a measure of what we are consuming. Quality of life, on the other hand, is the measure of how good your life is, not how big it is. A great meal instead of a super-sized meal. A Conserving Economy will necessarily have a lower standard of living because it doesn't consume as much as a Consuming Economy... it doesn't need to. As a matter of fact, a Conserving Economy might even look like it's in recession about half the time, but at the same time be a much more stable and delightful economy to live and work within. This is because recessions are signs of sickness in a Consuming Economy. But if they have any meaning at all in a Conserving Economy, they might even be construed as signs of health, because if your life is really good, then you need less additional stuff... and so you're buying less, but enjoying more.

the CONSERVING ECONOMY: FINANCE

Some segments of our current economy would clearly be less necessary in a Conserving Economy. Chief among these is the loan side of the finance sector, because when you need to spend less money to have a particular quality of life, then you don't need to borrow as much. But what's wrong with less debt, other than fewer loan officer jobs?

The flip side of the finance sector is the investment side: if your cost of living is reduced because your life-cycle costs go way down because of owning things that last, then you likely have more money to invest in your future security. And so we need more brokers and investment consultants.

the CONSERVING ECONOMY: INNOVATION

Another beneficiary of a Conserving Economy would likely be innovation. Here's why: When people are stretched to their limits maintaining their standard of living, their efforts are consumed with things pertaining to financial survival. They have little time for pursuing great ideas. But when they are freed from wall-to-wall survival demands, then they have time and energy that may be used for thinking "what if...?"

My own experience follows this track. Soon after architecture school, my wife Wanda and I decided to build what was intended to be a self-sufficient homestead. For a short while, our debt was low, so we had time to think about a better world. Our contribution was going to be a house on one acre that heated and cooled itself, and that fed our little family. The heating and cooling innovations included several items, including a system I called "cool tubes."

Here's the house we built. It got appraised at $25/square
foot because it had the audacity to try to heat itself instead of
having conventional heating equipment.

Unfortunately, the finance sector didn't know what to do
with us. The appraisers (we went through several of them)
were so flummoxed by the idea of a house with no heat pump
that their appraisals were ridiculously low, even though our
passive system would save thousands in utility costs. And so
we had to take two years building most of it ourselves to save

on labor, and we got as many credit cards as we could to buy the materials to finish the job.

As you might imagine, when a house is partially financed on credit cards, its owners must struggle mightily for several years. Nearly every moment was spent surviving. And I became completely invisible in the arena of innovation.

When the tax law changes of 1986 finally had their full impact on my employer, my job was downsized and I hung out my shingle in 1991 with the early 1990s recession in full swing. Several more years of survival mode ensued as I worked to build a business from the ground up. I continued to be com-

The full value of Seaside Institute events may never be known. Many New Urbanists first left their own little islands and plugged into the movement at symposia here.

pletely invisible to anyone interested in architecture or place-making innovation because I wasn't contributing any innovations. Wanda and I were merely surviving; nothing more.

Finally, however, we began to achieve a small measure of success towards the end of the 1990s. And that opened a small window of available time within the demands of keeping a small business afloat. The initiatives were tiny at first. We began the *Mooresville Collection* of homes designed for New Urbanist neighborhoods in 1996. Our *Catalog of the Most-Loved Places* began humbly at the beginning, with the photographing of a few lesser-known Alabama towns in 1997. The window opened a bit to include symposia at the Seaside Institute beginning in 1999, which led to the close relationships we enjoy to this day with many notable New Urbanists.

Our move to Miami Beach in 2003 was the culmination of years of house downsizing from 3,000 square feet to our current 747 square feet. And the early initiatives opened the door to high-value work we have enjoyed in recent years whereby I can work 7-10 days a month to pay the bills and spend the rest of my time writing books and working on new initiatives.

A Katrina Cottage

Some of these include the Katrina Cottages movement (more on that in Chapter 2.) Today, we're working on far too many cool things to list here. Our primary initiative, the Original Green, would have been impossible to advance in financial survival mode.

But a small window of uncommitted time can lead to small innovations, which leads to greater value of one's time, which leads to a bigger window for more innovation. All of this is made harder in a Consuming Economy, but easier in a Conserving Economy.

the CONSERVING ECONOMY *in* PRACTICE

And a Conserving Economy isn't just theory…Wanda and I are living it already. Our standard of living has shrunk notably over the past few years. Our new home is only a quarter of the size of our first one. We now have one car rather than two. We ride a bike to the grocery store. I walk to work. By the Consuming Economy standards of bigger and more, we must have fallen upon hard times. We must be failures.

But the Conserving Economy standards of quality of life tell a completely different story. We moved to paradise, otherwise known as South Beach. We don't have to fight traffic. We are healthier because we walk and bike everywhere. We save thousands by not needing as many cars. I could go on for pages, listing numerous ways our quality of life has gone up, but it's so good it would be embarrassing. Let's just say that we consider ourselves to be extremely fortunate for a quality of life that is far beyond what we ever deserved, even though many measures of our standard of living are reduced.

Quantity or Quality. More or Better. Consume or Conserve.
Because resources are finite, we must choose a path to prefer
one or the other.

4 ~ *the* ACHILLES HEEL *of* ARCHITECTURE

We cannot build a sustainable world without architects, but architecture today has a flaw that prevents sustainability. For nearly a century, much of the architectural profession has worked on the premise that if you want to be significant, your work must be unique. At first glance, this might appear to be good for the profession, and also to have nothing to do with sustainability. Neither are correct, as we shall see.

the NECESSITY *of* UNIQUENESS

The necessity of uniqueness seems to encourage creativity and invention. What could possibly be wrong with that? Architects explored most of the rational ways of doing Modernism by around the end of the 1950s. You may like them or you may not, but the works of Frank Lloyd Wright, Mies van der Rohe, Walter Gropius, Le Corbusier, Louis Kahn, Alvar Aalto, Adolf Loos, Eero Saarinen and their contemporaries clearly made sense, and could be explained to anyone that cared to listen.

Brutalism, arguably the trademark style of the Lost Generation of architects, typically turned hard, blank, unfriendly concrete faces to the street.

The next generation of Modernists were faced with a co-nundrum: whether to hold to the necessity of uniqueness even as unique but sensible Modernist architecture was getting harder to find, or instead to do things that didn't make sense. It is not so terribly unfair to characterize these architects as the "Lost Generation." Architecture during this era was not all bad, to be sure, but it included some of the most soulless, sterile architecture the world has ever seen. Brutalism, their signature style, even sounds like a condition to avoid.

A revolt against the Lost Generation started brewing in the 1970s. But as rebellions go, it wasn't long before there was a schism. Some of the rebels decided to be true to the necessity of uniqueness, even if that meant that their work might be irrational. This camp was composed primarily of architects who would go on to become today's "starchitects." The other camp of rebels chose instead to do things that made sense, even if those things were not unique. These architects went on to become today's New Urbanists and New Traditionalists.

Today, if you want to be significant in architectural circles, you must out-weird Frank Gehry. To be significant ten years from now, you'll have to out-weird the person that out-weirded Frank Gehry. As a result, today's architecture is in a death spiral towards the Wall of Terminal Weirdness, where things simply cannot get any stranger. What does any of this have to do with sustainability? And why is it important?

the IMPORTANCE *of* ARCHITECTURE *to* SUSTAINABILITY

Here's what architecture has to do with sustainability, and why it matters: According to the US Energy Information Administration (www.eia.doe.gov) buildings used 41% of all en-

*Architecture has developed in many ways around the world
to be sustainable in its regional conditions, climate,
and culture.*

ergy consumed in the US in 2008. Transportation consumed
28% and industry consumed 31% in 2008. This means architecture is responsible for the largest single chunk of American energy consumption. So it is inescapable that architecture
must play a major role in a sustainable future. Put another way,
sustainability cannot occur without architecture changing.

Today, millions of the brightest minds around the world are
working to figure out how we can live sustainably on earth
today. It's a really tough problem, and many of them have
been working for years to figure it out. I'm an optimist, and
believe they eventually will.

What is it? Where is the front door? And if it can't even tell people what kind of building it is or where the front door is, how can it tell people how to live sustainably?

When that day comes, will architects still insist on the necessity of uniqueness? How ridiculous would it be to think that any single architect could take the massive collection of ideas that will constitute the wisdom of sustainability and reinvent it all in their own personal style? If it took millions of the best minds years to figure it out, what chance does any

[46]

single architect have of re-making it all? This is a completely impossible task. Its futility should be obvious.

But even if that task wasn't futile, there's another equally unworkable problem: Architectural styles are like languages; specific patterns (the ways we build eaves, windows, etc.) are like words in that language. When an architect invents a new unique style, she invents an architectural language. How would it ever be possible to get everyone involved if we're speaking in a language they don't know? It is impossible to share the wisdom of sustainability that way.

Real sustainability must involve everyone, not just the specialists.

How to Fix It

We must be allowed to share wisdom! Pure and simple. Architecture must be able to pass wisdom down for generations in common languages if we are to build sustainably.

3 ~ *the* Fuzzy Carbon Focus

Focusing on the carbon footprint of a building is a recipe for failure. Why? The speed of life today tempts us at every turn to simplify things to a single variable. Who can blame us, with the exploding information bandwidths of our digital age? So complex issues get crunched into bumper stickers and sound bites. Focusing on carbon footprint may sound at first like precision, but it's actually blurring our vision of the bigger picture.

Global climate change is only the latest victim of over-simplification, having been reduced to the single issue of carbon emissions. And let's be clear: carbon dioxide levels in the atmosphere *are* important, because the great majority of scientists now agree that carbon dioxide levels are an indicator of global climate change. The problem isn't that carbon dioxide levels are unimportant, but rather that they are not a silver bullet. Why not? The focus on carbon creates fuzzy vision in several ways:

the CARBON FUZZINESS *of* EXTRAVAGANCE

Focusing on carbon dioxide alone lets us do all sorts of ridiculous things so long as the buildings can somehow be termed "carbon neutral." But does that mean it's really sustainable? Google "carbon-neutral McMansion" and you'll come back with more than 5,000 hits, for example. Real sustainability means keeping things going in a healthy fashion long into an uncertain future. The meltdown is a bitter reminder that keeping things going takes a lot more than just avoiding high utility bills. Will those McMansions be here in 300 years or more just because they have lower utility bills... compared to other equally extravagant houses?

the Carbon Fuzziness *of* Place

The fuzzy carbon focus also lets us design modest buildings located in auto-dominated places. While the buildings themselves might be carbon-neutral, the lifestyle is far from it because if you have to drive everywhere, then you're still responsible for putting lots of carbon in the atmosphere. Look at the building in the image below. How silly is it to trumpet buildings in auto-dominated places like this as carbon-neutral? Yet this is being done everywhere. Ignoring the context of the building while claiming carbon neutrality simply does not pass the smell test, nor does it meet the standard of common sense. We risk forfeiting the credibility of green standards by having fuzzy vision toward the carbon impacts of place.

*Boston City Hall won huge architectural acclaim when it
was built, but is now in danger of facing the wrecking ball
simply because it was never loved by the citizens.*

the CARBON FUZZINESS *of the* UNLOVABLE

The issue of lovable buildings will be dealt with at length
later, but it must be mentioned here, too, because the carbon footprint of a building is meaningless once its parts are
prematurely carted off to the landfill because it could not be
loved. Many architects are under the delusion that they know

[50]

what people *should* want, and that it's the responsibility of the public to learn how to properly appreciate their designs. But the citizens almost always beg to differ, and buildings are frequently demolished for no other real reason than the fact that they cannot be loved. Remember 7 ~ *the Fate of Ought-To?* Telling people they ought to love a building because it's carbon neutral has little chance of saving an unlovable building.

the Carbon Fuzziness *of* Offsets

The principle of carbon offsets sounds reasonable at first glance: Do all that you can, then pay someone else to do

The best sort of carbon neutrality comes from building lovably and durably, using techniques that allow the building to largely condition itself, so frugality comes naturally.

something good to offset the carbon you are emitting. But dig just a bit below the surface, and there are many problems.

One problem is the location of the offsetting activity. Someone rarely buys an offset they can see. In most cases, the offsetting activities are located offshore, often in developing countries on a different continent. As a result, the likelihood of the person or company buying the offsets ever seeing the offsetting activity is vanishingly small. So is the offsetting activity actually taking place?

"But wait," you ask, "If someone is spending thousands or even millions of dollars buying carbon offsets, don't they have a strong financial interest in making sure that the offsets are actually happening? Why should carbon offsets be any less interesting than anything else upon which you spend thousands or millions of dollars?"

Here's why: When you invest a large amount of money in something, you expect your investment to appreciate in value. When you spend a lot of money on a product, you expect it to operate as advertised. When you spend a lot of money on a service, you expect to be well-served. But what are you really buying when you purchase carbon offsets? To be blunt, you are paying someone to export your guilt. And so once the carbon offset has been purchased, you've received what you paid for: a conscience that doesn't bother you. As a matter of fact, digging too deeply into the carbon offset after you've purchased it actually undermines the purchase. Why? Because if you find out that the purveyor of the offset actually did exactly what they said they did, then the only thing you accomplished is to spend a lot of time and money to verify what you thought you already knew.

But if you find out that the purveyor of the offset was less than credible and the offset didn't actually happen as advertised, then you've just spent a lot of money to destroy the value of the clean conscience you thought you had purchased. Clearly, then, purchasers of carbon offsets have far less incentive to verify the quality of the offsets than they do to verify the quality of other investments, goods, and services that they purchase.

For a completely incisive parody of the concept of offsetting to carbon neutrality, check out www.cheatneutral.com. The premise of the website is that "When you cheat on your partner you add to the heartbreak, pain and jealousy in the atmosphere. Cheatneutral offsets your cheating by funding someone else to be faithful and NOT cheat. This neutralizes the pain and unhappy emotion and leaves you with a clear conscience." From that point, the website offers two avenues: "Are you a cheater? Cheatneutral can help you offset your indiscretions." Or, "Loyal and faithful? Become an offset project and get paid for not cheating." If this sounds ludicrous, check out the website. Its corollary to carbon offsets is stunning; you may be asking yourself which is most ridiculous, the cheating credits or the carbon credits, before you finish surfing.

The bottom line is that focusing on carbon footprint alone is a guaranteed losing strategy. Additionally, the potential for scandal in the carbon offset business is so great that it carries the risk of being one of the biggest swindling operations to date in the twenty-first century because the psychology of offset purchases does not encourage accountability. Carbon is clearly an essential part of the equation of sustainability, but it's only a part. That's the problem with the dilemma of sustainability ... there are many essential parts, and ignoring the others in favor of a single part will guarantee our failure. And we cannot afford to fail.

2 ~ *the* Supply-Side Focus

Sustainability cannot be achieved simply by buying more efficient stuff. Many things are being redesigned to be more efficient: better light bulbs, better cars, better heating and cooling equipment, and cleaner sources of electricity, for example. And by all means, we should support this. But these are all things that the manufacturers must do. In other words, they're supply-side: they're accomplished by those who supply us with the things that we use (and consume.)

Now, try this exercise: (1) Select any mechanically- or electrically-operated product type you can think of. (2) Use any common measure of sustainability, whether carbon footprint, miles traveled, net energy, etc. (3) Take the best assumptions of competent advocates for increases in efficiency or effective-

ness of the product type. (4) Compare the likely increases in efficiency to the best projections of increases in demand.

In most cases, you'll find that the demand will rise faster than the projected improvements in the product. So while the products are getting better, we're still using more energy and other resources in order to use those products. So we're going further in the hole all the time.

Take cars, for example. This chart shows the miles traveled on US streets and highways beginning in 1960. If you project the trend of the past half-century (business as usual) it follows the red line. How much can the supply side help? For the first time in 32 years, Congress increased the mandatory US fleet efficiency from 25 miles per gallon to 35 miles per gallon in 2007... to be effective in 2020. Better efficiency clearly helps, but by how much? Driving a car that is 10% more efficient uses the same amount of gas as driving 10% less. The yellow line on the graph shows the effect of the increased efficiency. The dilemma is obvious: even though the increased efficiency

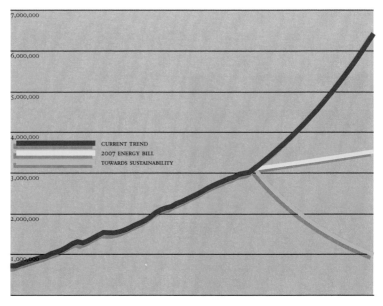

Data Source: US Department of Transportation, Federal Highway Administration. Values are millions of miles.

makes a big impact, the line is still rising, which means we'll still be burning more gas. And this chart shows the efficiency increasing at the same rate to 2030, even though the law only requires it until 2020.

And the problem is, we don't need to level off where we are now; we need to go *much* lower. In order to reach a level that most scientists would consider sustainable, we need to follow something close to the green line, and any knowledge-able engineer in the automotive industry will tell you that the green line simply isn't happening. That line represents the equivalent of reducing US driving to a trillion miles a year by 2030 (approximately the level in 1968) while the actual distance traveled in 2030 will actually be closer to 6 trillion miles. To burn gas equal to the green line while driving as much as we'll likely be driving, the average fuel efficiency in 2030 would have to be around 150 miles per gallon. Does any-one believe there's any chance whatsoever of this happening?

And that's only part of the problem. It's scary enough just looking at projections for the United States, but when you

consider that there are over two and a half billion people in China and India that are now moving from highly sustainable agrarian cultures to an industrial economy much like ours in the 1950s and 1960s, it's obvious that our supply-side focus cannot be a winning strategy. Everything only gets worse when we depend upon a supply-side strategy. To be clear, we must supply better stuff, but that *alone* won't do the job... it doesn't even come close.

the GIZMO GREEN

Gizmo Green is another way of explaining the supply side focus. Gizmo Green is based primarily on things that others can do for us: give us better machines to buy and better materials to buy and use in our buildings, and we'll achieve

sustainability. Or will we? We will see later in this book that Gizmo Green is a part of true sustainability, but only a very small part.

Gizmo Green, unfortunately, constitutes a huge percentage of today's sustainability discussion. Buy compact fluorescent light bulbs. Buy a Prius. Buy some bamboo... and everything will be okay. The solution to everything is to go shopping. Or is it really?

The Gizmo Green focus allows us to ignore huge essential facets of sustainability that have nothing to do with equipment or materials. For example, why are we even discussing the carbon footprint of a building if it is built somewhere that requires you to drive everywhere, as illustrated in *3 ~ the Fuzzy Carbon Focus*? Or what is the value of the carbon footprint of a building once its parts are carted off to the landfill because it could not be loved?

That's why Gizmo Green is, by itself, a losing strategy. The concerns of Gizmo Green are good, but only so long as they are incorporated into a much larger strategy that provides real sustainability.

the FALLACIES *of* EFFICIENCY

The first fallacy of efficiency is thinking that we're going to benefit from all those ef-ficiency gains. We won't. Why not? Roughly a century ago, Thomas Edison said "We will make electricity so cheap that only the rich will burn candles." A half-century later, Lewis L. Strauss, chairman of the Atomic Energy Commission, gushed over the apparent economy of nuclear power: "Our children will enjoy in their homes electrical energy too cheap to meter." He was famously wrong, of course, as Chernobyl and Three Mile

Island raised questions of whether providing nuclear power safely was a proposition too expensive to tolerate.

EFFICIENCY *vs.* DEMAND

So Edison was right, but not Strauss. What if both had been right? With electricity too cheap to meter, would you ever turn the lights off, except to sleep? Or let's look at it another way: if your light bulbs were so efficient that leaving them on would cost you very little, would you turn them off? If your car got 100 miles per gallon, why not drive further? This is the first fallacy of efficient: the more efficient a machine or fixture is, the less incentive there is to use it less. In other words, something that is 50% more efficient does not deliver 50% less energy use.

the EFFICIENCY *of* PLACE

The second fallacy of effi- ciency is believing that real- istic efficiency gains can cre- ate a sustainable world. As we saw at the beginning of this section, and as Jim Kunstler points out repeatedly in *The Long Emergency*, technology can only deliver so much, and it's not going to be enough. This highlights the fact that it's actually more effective to

*Our first South Beach car was a Mini like this. Our new
one is a convertible Smart. We don't drive much, but we have
fun when we do!*

change our minds (and then to change our behavior) than it is to change our gadgets.

My own experience is a good example. I once lived in a place that was almost completely unwalkable. Between the two of us, Wanda and I drove about 48,000 miles a year in two cars. We moved to Miami Beach in 2003 to work more

closely with the many New Urbanists here, and our driving
habits changed immediately because the place is so walkable.

We live five blocks from the office; I walk, while Wanda
bikes so she can carry our three miniature dachshunds in the
front basket so they don't make the trip a 30-minute sniffing
expedition. Our office is within two blocks of three neighborhood grocery stores, and our home is four blocks from
Whole Foods, so the front basket and two saddlebag baskets
on the bike are good for almost all grocery trips. Our bank is
five blocks from the office. The hardware store is two blocks
away; the post office is across the street. The drug store is two
blocks away. There must be dozens if not hundreds of restaurants within a five-minute walk. Yet once we moved here, I
lost 60 pounds because of all the walking.

Here's the building where we have our office: It has a cof-

fee shop on one end, a pub
on the other, a gym above,
and lots of other businesses in
between:

But I digress... the real
point here is efficiency. We
now crank the car roughly
twice a week, and drive less
than 6,000 miles per year.
That's *one eighth* as much as
we drove before. If we wanted
to achieve the same reduction
in gasoline use with a more
efficient car instead, while still
driving 48,000 miles a year,

we'd have to have a car that was 8 *times as efficient* as my Accord and Wanda's CRV. Or, in percentage terms, that's 800% as efficient. The Accord got around 30 miles per gallon; it would need to get about 240 miles per gallon to have the same effect. Clearly, that's impossible in the foreseeable future.

Almost everyone agrees that increasing the American fleet efficiency by 8% each year is nothing but a fantasy, or an impossible dream. But when we moved to South Beach, the effect was 100 times better (800/8) than the impossible dream of efficiency! Let that sink in for just a minute: *one hundred times better than efficiency's impossible dream!*

This is not to say that we should not have more efficient cars, machines, and light bulbs. Efficiency is fine if you want to ease your conscience, but it is a losing strategy for achieving sustainability. *If our behavior doesn't change, then our machines can't save us.*

And if our behavior does change, then those savings will dwarf the efficiency savings. And in my own experience, our behavior did not change because we suddenly felt that it was our duty to walk everywhere, but because it is so much fun to walk all over South Beach as a result of the way it's designed. Put another way, the best way to change behavior is with enticement.

I ~ *the* TWO *and a* HALF BILLION PEOPLE

Even if the US and Europe become massively more effi-cient, all the good we might hope to do in the upcoming decades is likely to be dwarfed by the problem of immensely large numbers. And whether you care deeply for the earth, or care only for your own financial well-being, this one is going to have a major impact.

Until now, the world's biggest ecological disaster was the American middle-class lifestyle. Sprawl, super-sizing, and slurping of the lion's share of the world's resources has had a huge impact, but that's about to change... because today, there are two and a half billion people living in China and India, who have until now lived within agrarian societies, consum-ing very few resources per person.

But now, China is industrializing, and India is skipping straight to the post-industrial economy, and the two and a half billion are moving off the land and into the cities, just as mil-lions of Americans did during the Great Decline. And as the two and a half billion move into the cities, they come face-

A megalopolis growing larger by the minute, and extending as far as the eye can see

to-face with images of something they may never have seen before: the American middle-class lifestyle. And they want it. And who are we to tell them they can't have it? What are the chances that they would listen? Actually, they've already answered the question in resounding fashion by adopting our lifestyle in mammoth proportions.

[65]

The two and a half billion have lived until now as peasants on the land, with very low ecological impact.

The problem is obvious: the environmental problems we have now get multiplied by more than nine: 2.8 billion (us plus them) versus 300 million (just us) in just a few years because there will be over nine times as many people trying to live the American middle-class lifestyle. Imagine in seven to ten years when a billion cars that don't even exist today get on the roads in China and India. What will that do to the price of gas? What will that do to air quality? What will that do to the global climate?

So the world's biggest ecological disaster is no longer the American middle-class lifestyle, but rather the export of the

[66]

Here's what the two and a half billion want now:
the inherently unsustainable American middle-class lifestyle.

*Low-impact agrarian lifestyles may soon be nothing more
than a memory for over two and a half billion people.*

image of the American middle-class lifestyle. We haven't even
begun to understand the impact of multiplying our problems
by nine. Is there any question as to whether it's time to find
better ways of solving these problems than what we're currently doing?

PART TWO
WHAT CAN WE DO?
THE TOP 10 BETTER WAYS OF BEING GREEN

Our problems go far beyond anything that could be considered "daunting." As a matter of fact, it is questionable whether humanity has yet faced a challenge to its future that compares to the scale of what lies ahead, except in disaster and alien movies. Look at any major chart of world conditions over the span of recorded human history, whether it be human population, energy usage, resource usage, atmospheric carbon dioxide, etc., and you will see immediately that there is an unprecedented skyrocketing of the chart in the past 200 to 300

[69]

Bubbles are enticing... until they burst.

years. Any reasonable person would have to conclude that we cannot continue on our present course without massive consequences... believing otherwise would give your friends cause for questioning your sanity. One definition of insanity is to believe that we can keep doing what we've been doing and somehow get different results. Zig Ziglar's take on the truth behind the Insanity Principle is "if you keep doing what you've been doing, you're going to keep getting what you've been getting."

But the Insanity Principle doesn't really cover the uncharted territory we're in now. I'd like to propose the Inverse Insanity Principle, which states that "another sign of insanity is to believe that you can do dramatically different things (modern consumption-dominated lifestyles) and somehow get the same result as before you did those dramatically different things."

These ideas aren't really new, however. A Jewish philosopher lumped both the Insanity Principle and the Inverse Insanity Principle into a single phrase nearly 2,000 years ago when he observed that "you reap what you sow."

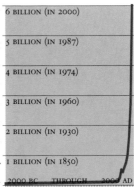

World Population. For perspective, do you see the tiny glitch a few centuries ago? That was the Black Death.

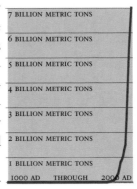

Total Carbon Emissions from Fossil Fuels. Source: CDIAC.

Atmospheric Carbon Dioxide.
Source: Scripps, ORNL, & IPCC

Worldwide Species Extinctions Per Year
Source: Encarta

"Bubble thinking" isn't new, either. Bubble thinking during the recent housing bubble that burst in 2008 and the dot com bubble that burst in 2000 serve as warnings against the irrational exuberance that would comfort us that "everything's OK..." when we're in completely uncharted waters, creating unprecedented conditions that have unknown effects.

Those are not the only bubbles we have seen... not by any stretch. Before them, there was the Asian financial bubble that burst in 1997, the Japanese asset bubble that burst in the 1980s, the Florida speculative building bubble that burst in 1926, the Railway Mania bubble of the 1840s, the Mississippi Company bubble of the 1720s, and the Tulip Mania bubble that burst in 1637, just to name a few. Bubbles are not new, but they all have something in common: they always seem to end in catastrophic fashion for the masses who are seduced by them.

These bubbles are characterized by the sharp spike in a single category of commodity, such as tulips, Florida real estate, or dot com stocks. But we now face a bubble like no other.

The Everything Bubble is unique because every chart of major global conditions is spiking or otherwise behaving as it has never done before in recorded human history. See the charts on the previous two pages? We could draw a dozen more that look very much like them.

What does this mean? At the very least, it points to the fact that humanity is entering an unprecedented era. It is not unreasonable to expect consequences of Biblical proportions; how can we look at the charts and rationally believe otherwise? Is there anything other than "bubble thinking" that would make us hope that everything's OK, and that, in the words of Jim Kunstler, we can "sleepwalk into the future"?

With that said, I must say that I am an optimist, and believe that our future and that of our children can be OK, but only if we do certain things to help build a more sustainable future. The actual plan for achieving that sustainable future is contained in the next chapter. This one lays out the top ten principles that should underlie any such plan. In other words, it paints a picture of the foundations of a sustainable future.

*Does it work? We shouldn't base green strategies on ideas
that don't work.*

10 *the* Things *that* Work should become our new measuring-stick. Real sustainability must be pragmatic, based simply on things that make sense in the long run.

9 *the* Six Realms *of* Green is the idea that while some sustainability strategies should be universal, others should be continental, or national, or regional, or even local. One size

clearly doesn't fit all, if we're looking for real sustainability.

8 *the* Green Country *to the* Green City looks at how we need to figure out how to live sustainably at all settings, from the most rural to the most urban.

7 *the* Simpler Way is a set of the greatest cost-control devices we no longer use... but we should, so we can afford to improve the performance of our buildings.

6 *the* Many Uses is making things do double-duty, triple-duty, or even more, so you can consume less.

5 *the* Source *of* Stuff means that materials that are harvested and processed nearer to where they are used are preferable.

4 *the* Expanded Comfort Range is the tolerance our ancestors them had to wider variations in their environment so the equipment doesn't run all the time.

3 *the* Localized Operations are things that have a smaller circle of effect. Conditioning a smaller area saves energy.

2 *the* Sharing *of* Wisdom is essential if we hope to achieve the most important principle, which is...

1 *the* Involvement *of* Everyone is something we simply cannot do without. If we are to live sustainably, we must all do differently... and we must do so because we *want* to do differently, not just because we have to.

Now let's get to the details...

10 ~ *the* THINGS *that* WORK

Our sustainability standards should be completely pragmatic. In other words, "do these things work?" Pragmatism is the standard of nature: If it works, it lives on. If it doesn't, it disappears from the face of the earth.

The cows and the cranes in the image below are one of the countless cooperative relationships in nature where two or more species help each other as they go about their daily lives. Life as we know it arguably would not exist without these relationships. Their standard is very simple: they each accomplish something good for each other.

Similarly, our question when examining a supposedly green thing should be: "What good does it accomplish?" Walking rather than driving, for example, accomplishes many obvious green things. Far too often, however, sustainability becomes a religion of sorts, where decisions are based more on faith than on the things that work. And the faith that is required is faith in a "green expert," faith in a company, or faith in an interest group of some sort. Have they earned our faith?

*Near or far? We are equally mistaken to believe that all
things sustainable are universal as to believe that all things
sustainable are local.*

9 ~ *the* Six Realms *of* Green

Sustainability is more often a function of the region, but
that's not always true. We must have some strategies that work
all over the world, while we need the nimbleness of other
strategies developed for a particular place. Here's a framework

for how these strategies can interact with each other to form a sustainable whole:

A pattern is simply something that happens again and again. Towns and buildings are made of languages of many patterns, from the ways that eaves are built in a particular place, to the region's most favorite ways of building a square.

This book organizes patterns into six Realms, from the smallest extent (the work of one person) to the largest (the universal.) The First Realm contains Personal Patterns. The Second Realm contains Local Patterns. The Third Realm contains Regional Patterns. The Fourth Realm contains National Patterns. The Fifth Realm contains Continental Patterns. The Sixth Realm contains Universal Patterns. Each realm has important and unique sustainability implications.

the FIRST REALM ~ PERSONAL PATTERNS

Every great idea begins with the single person who first conceives it. If it's an idea about a better way of building a building or a town, and if the person is convinced the idea is good enough, then they attempt to build it. If successful, they build it again. Because anything that is repeated again and again becomes a pattern, and because it is associated with the person who conceived the idea, it is a Personal Pattern. Anyone familiar with architecture should have no doubt that the image above is from a Frank Gehry building. Those are his patterns. Without the First Realm, we could not advance. But there is a problem with the Personal Patterns of the First Realm: they have no life of their own. This is because the patterns die with their originator if nobody copies them and they remain in the First Realm.

The First Realm is where invention occurs. We cannot live sustainably without invention, because conditions on earth change, and what will we do if we don't yet have an answer to a new condition? Some feel like we should simply go back to the 15th century, because people lived sustainably back then.

But we're not 15th century people anymore, so that clearly would not work. We must have a 21st century sustainability solution, because we can't simply forget everything we've learned since medieval times. So invention is essential. And it's essential (as we'll see later) that millions of people participate in the invention. Only then can we have real sustainability: when everyone is thinking about how to live better, creating a bubbling stew of innovation by millions of minds.

the Second Realm ~ Local Patterns

Sometimes, a Personal Pattern will resonate with others who see it, and they say "I want that on my house..." (or my shop, or my town, according to the scale of the pattern.)

And so they repeat it nearby, and it becomes a Local Pattern. Once a pattern spreads beyond its originator, a curious thing happens: it takes on a life of its own and can persist for decades, centuries, or occasionally millennia after its originator is dead and maybe even forgotten. In this way, it can be considered to be a living thing.

This is where living traditions begin; we will discuss them in more detail later in *1 ~ the Involvement of Everyone.* So while great ideas must begin as a Personal Pattern of the First Realm, they must also graduate to the Second Realm to have any chance of delivering sustainability.

Too many green decisions? The Second Realm localizes them, spreading the load.

The Second Realm is the testing ground of all that First Realm innovation, because patterns graduate to the Second Realm only when other people find them resonant or worthwhile. If they don't resonate, they don't graduate. First Realm patterns only need an inventor; Second Realm patterns require a community to test the ideas. The Second Realm is essential to sustainability because without this filter, there would be too many ideas to evaluate at the national or continental levels. We would choke on too many green choices.

the Third Realm ~
Regional Patterns

Often, Local Patterns (Second Realm) catch the eye of
travelers who are residents of
the same region. If the pattern is well-tuned to the regional conditions, climate,
and culture, then they are
likely to say "we love this...
and we want to adopt it into
our family of regional traditions." The process of adoption of
patterns into the Third Realm (Regional Patterns) illustrates
the fact that a living tradition is not made up of historical

artifacts as some would suppose, but rather, of things that
are worthy of love. Historical
artifacts no longer commonly produced are the prod-
ucts of traditions that were
once alive, but are now dead.
Third Realm patterns can be
thought of as making up the
regional dialect of a language
of architecture (more on this
in a moment.)

Third Realm patterns re-
spond to regional conditions,
climate, and culture. More of
the patterns of sustainability

occur in the Third Realm of Regional Patterns than in any other realm. While some Second Realm patterns are only appropriate to the locality where they were developed, many have a broader application and eventually graduate to the Third Realm.

A great example is the Charleston Single House (pictured below,) known everywhere except Charleston as the Charleston Sideyard. It is a house that turns its short face to the street, and its long face to a side garden. Front streets are the ones that most buildings front upon; they're where the doorbells are, in other words. The front streets in Charleston run generally North to South because of the shape of the peninsula the city is built upon. Because most lots are slender and deep rather than wide and shallow, this means that the short street face of the lot usually faces East or West.

The long South face usually has a long verandah to shade the wall in summer when the sun is high in the sky, but let in the low winter sun.

The North face has few if any windows, so as to not intrude upon the goings-on in your neighbor's side garden. This prac-

tice is known as "North Side Manners" in Charleston, meaning that if you have any manners, your house won't violate the privacy of your neighbor's garden.

The prevailing Southwest summer breezes cool the verandahs, while the cold Northwest winter wind is shielded by the mass of the house, extending the usable season of the verandah.

This pattern developed in Charleston, but has spread in recent decades all over the South because conditions are not so different in other parts of the region. Much like a healthy species will spread to adjacent compatible habitat, a Second Realm pattern that is applicable beyond the confines of the locality of the locality where it developed will spread to the region, becoming a Third Realm pattern and carrying its green intelligence with it.

the FOURTH REALM ~ NATIONAL PATTERNS

Occasionally, patterns are so resonant that they are adopted by an entire nation. While Regional Patterns (Third Realm) can be considered to make up the regional dialect of architecture and place-making, Fourth Realm patterns make up the national language of architecture and place-making. These languages are not the same as spoken languages, but there are certain striking similarities that are very helpful in understanding

*Nationally-understood forms include the colonnade
surrounding the plaza in Spain*

them. For example, individual patterns can be thought of
as words. And just as there are words in many languages for
"apple," with variations of regional dialects, so too are there
patterns in many architectural languages for "eave," complete
with countless Third Realm variations of the regional dialects.
Because Fourth Realm (national) patterns are broader than

any particular region's conditions, climate, or culture, they are most likely to express national aspirations or self-image, and contain within them traces of the history of the culture. Put another way, they often hold the memory of the culture.

The sustainability of the Fourth Realm is hardest to understand. This is because Fourth Realm patterns don't yet span continents like patterns do in the Fifth Realm, nor do they have the obvious green benefits of many Third Realm patterns. So does this Realm really have anything to do with sustainability? Yes. Here's two ways that Fourth Realm patterns can help make a nation sustainable:

Efficiency occurs when people don't have to stop and think about what they're doing. Fourth Realm patterns tell people how to use the town. They don't have to read the signs because they can literally read the town, if it's full of Fourth Realm patterns. But the greenest aspect of Fourth Realm patterns is the fact that they carry with them the hopes, aspirations, and national identity of a culture. What does this have to do with sustainability? Today, all except the most hopeless and impoverished cultures must aspire to be green. Why is this?

Many green advocates don't want to publicize this, but the best indicator of a green lifestyle is extreme poverty. If you're barely scraping out an existence on a tiny piece of land, then you're probably not generating a lot of garbage, or having other big impacts on the planet.

But for the rest of us, it's not so easy being green. We have to want to... with great vigor. That's where the Fourth Realm patterns come in. If our Fourth Realm patterns express our aspirations to be green, then we actually have a chance. As we'll see later, sustainability only happens when everyone is involved; it's not something that a few specialists can deliver. So deciding to be green individually isn't enough; we must also decide to be green as a nation. And Fourth Realm patterns can help establish that green national self-image.

the FIFTH REALM ~ CONTINENTAL PATTERNS

The Fifth Realm is the highest level of refinement to which anyone can elevate any pattern. Because of this, the Fifth Realm is the home of most of the patterns of each continent's classical tradition. In the case of Western Classicism, these patterns actually spread from Europe and now form the primary classical traditions of North America, and South America, in addition to Europe. (The classical tradition of Asia, for example, is far different.)

The myth of origins of the Corinthian order, related by Vitruvius, illustrates the rare instance where a single trained hand, in one brilliant stroke, can elevate a simple vernacular expression from the First Realm of Personal Patterns all the way to the Fifth Realm of Continental Patterns. Vitruvius tells of the sculptor Callimachus walking through the outskirts of Corinth about 2,500 years ago, where he happened across a tomb of a young girl. Her nurse had taken a few of the precious things of her life and put them in a basket, then put a roofing tile over the basket to shield them from the rain.

Over time, acanthus plants sprouted at the base of the basket, their leaves curling out as they grew up to meet the tile. Callimachus, the story goes, was so moved that he refined the nurse's simple expression into the Corinthian capital, which has persisted across the millennia.

Fifth Realm patterns change more slowly than all the others in the preceding realms. Many of these patterns have persisted

[87]

for millennia. How is it possible for a pattern to contribute to sustainability if it doesn't change? This question leads to the Novelty Paradox: Sustainability requires things that can be kept going in a healthy way long into an uncertain future. Keeping something going for centuries implies that it doesn't change much. But we can't be sustainable if we're not adaptable. Adaptation requires new things. So how can we, at the same time, keep something going for centuries and also adapt to new conditions?

Fifth Realm patterns clearly accomplish the former; Western Classicism has existed for more than 2,500 years. But Fifth Realm patterns, if understood as a language rather than a completed novel or textbook, can also be used to say things that have never been said before, whereas a novel or textbook is fixed in time the instant the ink dries. This, I believe, is the key to unlocking the Novelty Paradox: a process can do it; a product is completely impotent to do so.

This means that if Classicism (or more broadly, the most refined expressions of each continent) are understood as inalterable canons, fixed in time, then they are completely incapable of having any beneficial impact on the problem of sustainability because they cannot change. If, however, they are understood as languages that can say innumerable things, then they instantly morph from fixed-in-stone portraits of antiquity to adaptable tools that should be key to sustainability, because they last so long. Putting the book proposition another way, a book is fixed in time the instant the ink hits the paper, but a language that uses the exact words found in the book can be used to say things that have never been imagined before. Fifth Realm patterns benefit, therefore, when used as a language.

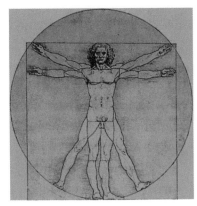

the Sixth Realm ~
Universal Patterns

Just like a smile or a laugh needs no explanation to any human on earth, the allure of hot coals of fire on a cool evening, the soothing breath of a cool ocean breeze in the tropics, or the assurance of an obviously durably-built beam need no expounding, either... they simply feel right... to any human. We know it's what we need.

What are the Universal Patterns of the Sixth Realm? First of all, they are the patterns that do not change. Some call this the Eternal Realm because of their permanence. They are things like the habitational comforts hardwired into all humans, our resonance with the natural laws of gravity and thermodynamics, and our resonance with rational proportions like 1:1, 4:3, and 3:2, and irrational proportions like the square root of 2

*When deciding which way to turn with a design, don't forget that
the universal patterns cast the broadest net, affecting everyone.*

and the Golden Mean. Most people cannot explain proper proportions; they simply have a comfort that all is right.

The Sixth Realm is the second-largest home of the patterns of sustainability, just behind the Third Realm of Regional Patterns. The Sixth Realm is where our humanity is most evident because this is where we are most like one another. What human doesn't gravitate to a crackling fire on a winter evening, or to the cooling murmur of a fountain of water on a scorching late-summer afternoon? These things aren't particular to any culture; rather, they're the things our species does when confronted with these conditions. These are things that we call "human habitational comforts."

And who doesn't gravitate to forms that reflect our own human form in some way? What's the first thing you do when you look at a photograph that includes you? You look at yourself, of course! We're hard-wired to look for things that reflect us, including things that reflect the shape of the human body. While many of today's architects may pooh-pooh symmetry, almost everyone else sees in it a reflection of the basic horizontal arrangement of the human face and body. We also resonate with forms, such as columns, that are arranged vertically like we are, with a top (head, or capital) a body (shaft) and bottom (base, or feet.) The most-loved buildings are usually arranged in this way, from the shape of the entire building all the way down to the smallest detail, such as the baseboards.

Sustainability benefits when we are able to stack the deck in our favor by designing places and buildings humans are hard-wired to love. If we under-
stand architecture as nothing more than fashion and style, then it's not possible to even anticipate the next fashion cycle, so sustainable buildings are impossible. But the Sixth Realm patterns empower us to design places and buildings that, even in an unimaginable future several centuries from now, people will still be predisposed to resonate with and sustain further and further into the future.

A pristine natural environment

8 ~ *the* GREEN COUNTRY *to the* GREEN CITY

American environmentalism makes a fundamental error by defining pristine wilderness as the ideal, placing humans apart from nature, and concluding that nature would be better off without us. Europeans don't make this error, because there's no untouched wilderness left to protect there.

A vibrant built environment

Extreme city-lovers sometimes make the opposite mistake. Because many metrics of environmental impact are better for city-dwellers than for those in the suburbs (less driving, etc.,) they argue that the city is the ideal condition, and that humans shouldn't live elsewhere. Interestingly, the city-lovers' view is similar to the American environmentalists' view in this respect: by saying that we should all live in the city, it also

[93]

implies that we should stay away from the wilderness and therefore not spoil it.

Both of these views are incorrect for two reasons: because each view tries to make a single setting the ideal to the exclusion of all others, and because each view misrepresents the proper relationship of humans and nature. We'll address the single-setting problem in a moment, but let's first look at the relationship of humans to nature. This book firmly takes that position that humans should be seen as being a part of nature, not apart from nature. How can this be?

the RELATIONSHIP *of* HUMANS *and* NATURE

Let's start by comparing a natural place and a man-made place. Look closely at the image below. What do you see? This appears to be a completely natural scene, with no evidence of human intervention. What are the components of this scene? We can see green things that are living. We can also see dead wood that was once alive, but no longer is. And we can see rocks that have never been alive. And we can assume that various creatures probably scurry, slither, or crawl across this scene from time to time, even though none of them appear to be here at this moment.

Now look at the image on this page. What do you see? This is clearly a place that has been built by humans. What are the components of this scene? We can see green things that are living. We can also see things that were once alive, but no longer are, like the wood in the shutters, windows, and doors. And we can also see brick, stone, and metal that has never lived. And we can assume that various creatures (mostly humans, but probably dogs, cats, birds, and other creatures) run or walk across this scene from time to time. Matter of fact, if you look closely, you'll see that one fellow is in the picture now, walking along the sidewalk under the gallery.

So it's clear that both the natural place and the man-made place have some of the same categories of materials. Their arrangement, however, is completely different. The natural scene is arranged by forces of nature, while the man-made

scene is arranged by human hands for the shelter, comfort, pleasure, and convenience of those that live there.

But we're not the only creatures that make homes for ourselves. Birds build nests. Bees build hives. Beavers build lodges on ponds they've created by damming streams. Rabbits build underground warrens, as do many other burrowing creatures. Bears find and inhabit caves. Spiders build webs. Ants build

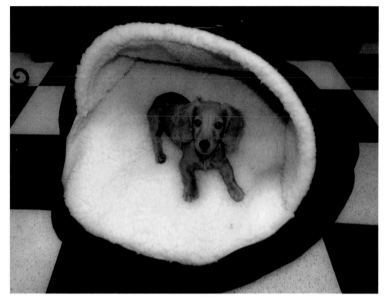

Sally in her dog-cave bed

anthills. Many creatures build or find their own particular type of home. The homes that humans build are more elaborate, to be sure, but we are by no means the only creatures that modify the natural world to shelter and protect ourselves.

Some creatures are exceptionally clever because rather than building their own homes, they entice other creatures to build homes for them. This is a picture of my puppy Sally. She was only three months old when this picture was taken, but she's such a sweetheart that I bought this bed for her. And that's not even half the story, because really, my whole house and garden is hers, too. Really clever.

Nature, then, is shaped not only by natural forces like gravity, wind, water, and sunshine, but also by all the creatures that make their homes there... including humans. But humans have built many horrific landscapes in recent years. It's an impossible stretch to say that a coal power plant or an auto junkyard is a part of nature, isn't it?

What standard can we use to distinguish between places like the hamlet below, that can reasonably be seen as being a natural part of the landscape, and places like a boarded-up suburban strip mall, which nobody would ever consider to be a part of nature?

How about using the standard of sustainability: "keeping things going in a healthy way long into an uncertain future." A "healthy way" means that we should leave it as good as we found it. This hamlet, for example, may be a fair exchange for the forest it replaced. A junkyard clearly is not. Of course, like the hamlet that has likely been inhabited for centuries, it's better yet not to leave it at all. A sustainable place is a place where you want to stay, not a place that you want to leave. So

Without a doubt, this place is worse than the field or forest that was bulldozed to make way for it, even before it failed. And it failed so quickly! Just look at how young most of the trees are.

many places built in recent decades are so bad that we discard them as quickly as possible, littering the landscape with cast-off places that are far worse than the places they replaced.

It's clear that the error of the American environmentalists' view of nature stems from our recent track record of building horrific places and quickly discarding them. That truly does spoil the environment. Interestingly, there has not been pristine wilderness in Europe for a very long time, so environmentalists there are much more likely to see humans as a part of nature rather than apart from nature like their American counterparts.

[98]

the Problem *of* Single Settings

The other problem identified earlier is the problem of establishing a single ideal environmental setting whether it's wilderness or city, and then trying to make everything else fit into that setting. People don't live in only one type of settlement. We need to know how to build the city sustainably, and also its suburbs, and also the countryside around them. We need to know how to build towns sustainably. We need to know how to build villages sustainably. And we need to know how to build hamlets sustainably, too.

It isn't just the cities, suburbs, towns, villages, and hamlets that need to be sustainable. All of the parts of those cities, suburbs, towns, villages, and hamlets need to be built in a sustainable way, too.

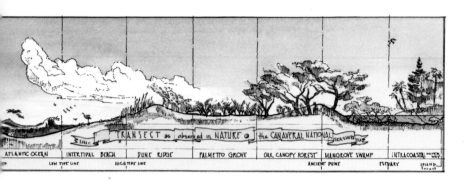

A Natural Transect. Illustrated by James Wassell.

the TRANSECT

The best tool available today for building all of the parts of cities, towns, villages, and hamlets in a sustainable way is a set of ideas known as the Transect. It was originally developed a century ago as a management tool for the natural environment. The Natural Transect illustrated above shows a series of adjoining habitats. Each has its own set of conditions, and its own set of plants and animals that thrive there. For example, sea oats thrive on the dune, but would die in the ocean.

In the late 1990s, New Urbanist planner Andrés Duany realized that the Transect could also be applied to human habitat. The Transect of the human habitat begins at T1, which is most rural, and runs to T6, which is most urban. Specific Transect zones are:

T1 NATURAL: This zone is untouched nature, or a park designed with no apparent human hand. Nobody lives here

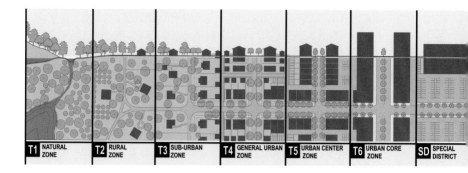

A Transect of the Built Environment.
Source: Duany Plater-Zyberk & Company

except the forest ranger. T1 could be dangerous; something might bite you, or might even eat you.

T2 RURAL: This zone is largely agricultural; it is made up mainly of farms, orchards, and meadows. The human hand can be seen here, but only very lightly, like a fence across the land, or a country road disappearing in the distance.

T3 SUB-URBAN: This zone is found primarily near the edges of neighborhoods, where the houses are spread more thinly. Large swaths of T3 are the main ingredient of many suburbs, which often suffer from having too much T3.

T4 GENERAL URBAN: This zone makes up much of the fabric of good in-town neighborhoods. Trees line the streets, which are flanked with fences with porches behind them. Townhouses and occasional corner stores can be found in T4.

T5 URBAN CENTER: Think of T5 as Main Street, with bustling sidewalks fronted by shops and restaurants with apartments above. Buildings sit tight to each other in T5, with offices, townhouses and apartment buildings on less busy streets.

T6 URBAN CORE: This zone exists in larger cities, but not towns or villages. This is where the buildings are the largest, the lights are the brightest, and things are happening until late at night.

Each Transect zone provides certain unique attributes and has certain needs. For example, we'll see later that if we want to build sustainable places, then most of the people need to be able to make a living where they're living. There are plenty of places to make a living in T5, but not in the less urban zones. It's clear, then, that sustainable places need to have some T5 in nearly every neighborhood, or at least in the adjacent neighborhood. But T5 has several special needs. For example, if there's not enough traffic (whether pedestrians, bikers, or cars) then it will starve because the businesses won't have enough customers. Once we know the important attributes and needs of each zone, the Transect allows us to very intelligently calibrate the sustainability of a place.

A cottage built using the Simpler Way.

7 ~ *the* Simpler Way

Humanity has, for almost all of recorded history, had an excellent way to build simply and control costs, but we discarded this method in most places roughly a century ago. Today, we seem bent on getting the look we want, even if it means we have to build with vinyl and duct tape.

The simpler way is known in some architectural circles as the Classical-Vernacular Spectrum. The most classical building in a state or province might be the state capitol or the state supreme court building. The most vernacular building may be a simple barn. Everything else is somewhere in between these two ends of the Spectrum. I'll explain more about the Spectrum later, but first, let's look at how we're building now.

THROWAWAY BUILDINGS *and* IMAGE GOO

Most of us living today have spent our entire lives in the era of "ticky-tacky houses" and throwaway buildings, so it's hard to even imagine how the simpler way worked. How does today's method work? Developments most likely begin in the offices of the marketing strategist, who comes up with

an image of the place. Maybe they call it Fox Run, and infuse the marketing package with naturalistic pictures. But of course, what Fox Run really means is "the place where the foxes will never run again." Or maybe it's a more refined image, like Georgian Estates, with pictures of fine brick buildings from the days of King George III. The specific image is unimportant... the point is that a place today starts with an image. Here's why that's a problem:

As the quality of the marketing strategist's work gets better and better, the chances of the developer being able to execute the image gets worse and worse. Here's why: If the image in the marketing package is vague, then it's easier to build in a way that occasionally comes close to fulfilling the marketer's promise. But if the image is powerful, then it evokes strong connections with images of ideal places in our minds. Because the image in our mind is potent, we know without doubt when the developer has failed to build to the image.

Portofino, shown on these pages, has been used as a development image countless times, yet there is still only one Portofino. The better the image created by the marketing consultant, the more miserable the failure of the developer will be when the place doesn't measure up.

And it isn't just *that* they fail, it's *how* they fail that is so regrettable. Because the development image rarely squares up with the best and most sustainable ways of building in a place, the developer is reduced to using the region's normal construction methods to build the building shell, then slathering architectural "image goo" all over it. In most cases, the image goo is cheap plastic, foam, or other stuff that is all too often a sad and hideous fake of the material it is intended to represent. Buildings made in this way are far too easy to discard at some point in the not-too-distant future. Clearly, throwaway buildings, even if less expensive to build, are unsustainable.

SUSTAINABILITY *versus* CONSTRUCTION COST

Sustainability is about much more than Gizmo Green, but

unless you're building in a place where natural methods can do the whole job of conditioning a building, then more efficient machines are essential. And better machines are almost always more expensive machines. Within a fixed construction budget, something's gotta give. In tough economic times such as the ones during which this book is being written, people usually choose the long, slow bleeding of monthly utility bills over up-front costs for energy equipment that would dramatically reduce or even eliminate the utility bills.

In order to buy the energy equipment, we must find savings elsewhere in the budget in most cases. The Classical-Vernacular Spectrum is the most powerful cost-control device in the history of human construction. As a matter of fact, it has created more affordable housing than any other method ever devised. It's high time to employ it once again... and put away the architectural image goo once and for all.

the Classical-Vernacular Spectrum *and* How It Works

The Classical-Vernacular Spectrum drives the Simpler Way and it works in an entirely different way from the throwaway buildings. First, it is based upon the best ways of building in a particular region. This makes image goo unnecessary because you don't have to fake anything. Next, it is infinitely adjustable based on the needs of each building. Need something more affordable? Fine... just dial it down the Spectrum a bit. Need something more refined? Just dial it up. And it's highly explainable to everyone from homeowners to builders to framers to masons, so that everyone understands why we build this way in this place. It's not just about something as fleeting as architectural fashion; rather, it's much more durable, and is characterized simply as "this is how we build here." It's not a style; it's what works best, for here and for us.

The classical end of the Classical-Vernacular Spectrum is the most refined architecture, and is very broad, spreading across entire continents. Europe, North America, and South America all share Western Classicism as their classical ideal. The most refined architecture of Asia or the Middle East, on the other hand, is a very different thing although the principle remains the same. But for the purposes of this discussion, let's look at the Classical-Vernacular Spectrums of Europe and the Americas, although Original Green principles work in exactly the same way in Asia and the Middle East, too.

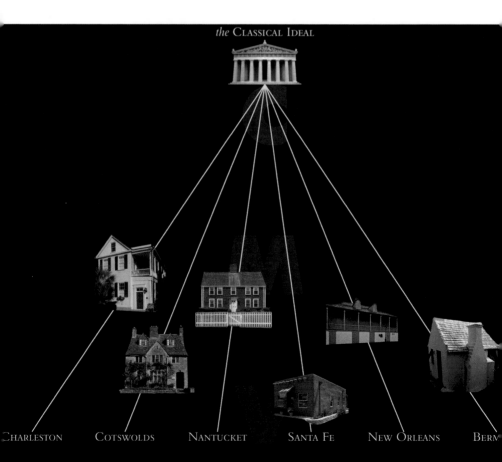

the CLASSICAL IDEAL

CHARLESTON   COTSWOLDS   NANTUCKET   SANTA FE   NEW ORLEANS   BERM

While many cultures of Europe and the Americas have long shared the same classical ideal for their most refined architecture, the vernacular end of the spectrum varies widely, as illustrated in the diagram on the opposite page. Each of the six places shown once had strong living traditions of place-making and building-making based on regional conditions, climate, and culture.

the Regional Conditions

Regional conditions include things like topography: is it a mountainous region, a coastal plain, or a prairie region? The most sustainable ways of building are different in each. What are the most readily available building materials in the region? This matters more as we try to find closer sources of materials with which to build. And what natural risks does the region face? People living in places frequented by hurricanes need to build in a certain way in order to have a good chance of

surviving them, while people living in earthquake zones have different concerns. Some regions face conditions so severe that you can't build strongly enough to endure them, such as tornadoes or volcanic eruptions. In those places, your only choice is to simply rebuild unless you choose to relocate elsewhere. But most other conditions are survivable if the architecture is smart enough.

the REGIONAL CLIMATE

The region's climate is the most obvious source of sustainability patterns. Places that are hot and humid need far different architecture from places that are cold and dark, or places that are hot and dry. Some regional green patterns have to do with ways of either welcoming the warmth of the sun

in cooler places (or in cooler times of the year in temperate places) or excluding its heat in hotter places (or hotter times of the year in temperate places, of course.) Other regional green patterns deal with moisture: In dry places, they collect water for many uses. In wet places, the bigger concern is getting the water of torrential rains away from the building so the building doesn't deteriorate and so the water doesn't damage the surrounding landscape.

Humidity is another source of green patterns. In dry places, rooms often cluster around enclosed courtyards to protect them against the wind, so that fountains and pools can create a more moist micro-climate than the surrounding bone-dry landscape. The architecture of humid regions finds ways of letting air flow freely through to lessen unhealthy growth of mold and mildew. Daylight is also a concern; places frequented by bright sunshine need shady environments where people can work, while places that are frequently cloudy and dark use many methods of enticing daylight into the buildings. The wind is another source of green patterns, because a cooling summer breeze is very welcome, whereas a cold winter wind is something to be deflected away. And in some places such as mountainous regions, the wind can be so strong most of the time that homes and workplaces always need to be shielded.

the Regional Culture

The human culture of the region can influence places and buildings in a number of ways. Some are as simple as color preferences, which help determine whether buildings are loved or viewed as odd foreign objects. Think of how strange a brightly-colored Guatemala courtyard house would look sitting side-by-side on the street with the stone houses of a Cotswold

*Antigua Guatemala: an architecture of Spanish colonial
culture adapted to the climate and conditions (earthquakes,
available materials, etc.) of Central America*

village in England, for example. Other regional cultural in-
fluences can have a more basic effect. Regional skill sets are
a classic example. Some still remain even today. For example,
masonry buildings finished in stucco are still fairly affordable
in Miami because that's the way people build there. Even
Habitat for Humanity builds that way, because their volun-
teers know how. But in the mid-South, stucco on masonry is
very expensive because few people know how to do it. Once,
nearly all the parts of a building depended on regional skill
sets. That may happen again as transportation costs rise.

the Classical Convergence *and* Sustainability

So the regional conditions, climate, and culture create regional vernacular traditions as varied as the regions, but the Classical-Vernacular Spectrum of each region converges on the classical ideal as we move up the spectrum. What's useful about that?

There's at least one highly useful thing about this from a green building perspective: Most places in the US didn't have time to develop a robust Original Green living tradition between the arrival of European settlers and the beginning of the Thermostat Age. The Thermostat Age began when mechanical equipment replaced natural methods of conditioning buildings, allowing our needs to be met at the touch of a button, and freeing our buildings from the responsibility to

condition themselves. Native Americans had strong living traditions in most places, but those were discarded by the European settlers, illustrating why culture is an essential part of the equation.

The American places shown in the diagram on page 108 are some of the exceptions because they were settled so early. But for the others, how do we go about figuring out what the regional vernacular would have been had it had time to develop?

This is far more of an art than a science, but one way is to look at some of the best classical work in the region. Because good classical work must be done by a trained and thoughtful hand, there's a good chance that if we look closely, we can see ways that the building diverges a bit from the classical ideal. Does it have more porches than what might be expected? How do its windows diverge in size, proportion, or count? What materials are used in its construction? Every place that the building diverges from the classical ideal is a potential hint at what the non-existent regional vernacular should possibly look like. And when we get to the vernacular end of the Classical-Vernacular Spectrum of the region, we'll find the greenest architecture of the place.

the QUESTIONS

Two questions arise from this: Are we saying that highly classical architecture isn't so green? And if the Native American architecture was so green, why not look to it for inspiration?

The Native American traditions of most regions are so organic that our culture, at least for today, would veto them. How many people do you know who would live in a teepee? Or a lodge built of sticks and branches? Architecture of the desert Southwest is an exception, as it borrows much from Native American traditions.

As for the greenness of highly classical buildings, clearly, they're not so attuned to the regional climate, but highly classical buildings are usually built strongest of all, able to withstand the harshest conditions. For example, most of the highly classical buildings of the Gulf Coast were built of stone, and were untouched by Hurricane Katrina, even though lesser buildings all around them were demolished. And architecture at the top of the Spectrum is often the highest expression of the culture of that place, so while they respond less to the regional climate, they come through in spades in response to the regional culture and often the regional conditions.

Consider these aspects of responding to regional climate: highly refined public buildings such as cathedrals or courts

 aren't places that you live, but rather places where you go for a limited time, then return home. Plus, you don't get undressed there to bathe, change clothes, or to go to bed. Before the Thermostat Age, people would simply bundle up if they were going there in winter. In a Long Emergency of reduced energy sources, like Jim Kunstler writes of, they could potentially do so again. Another type of highly classical building is the man-

sion of extremely wealthy people. No matter what the cost of energy is, the wealthiest people will always be able to buy it. But there simply aren't enough of these mansions in most places to make a blip on the energy consumption of the region, so as long as the people inhabiting them are OK with their utility bills, their impact on society at large is minimal.

6 ~ *the* MANY USES

If we hope to stem the tide of consumption, then we need to learn how to design and build things that have many uses

Katrina Cottage VIII, shown here on temporary display
(which is why it's on non-permanent foundation supports)

Katrina Cottage VIII interior before furnishing

again. In other words, double- or triple-duty is just the starting point. Today, we've not only lost this ability, but now, we have extras of everything instead.

It begins at the scale of the neighborhood. Because there's no neighborhood coffee shop within walking distance, some homes now have a "cafe" in the kitchen, with a cute little awning over the espresso machine. Because there's no neighborhood cinema, people feel that they need a home theatre. Because there are no parks within a couple blocks, people need big back yards for the kids.

But it's not all the neighborhood's fault. Kids' bedrooms in many homes sold just before the Meltdown were better-appointed than master suites a generation before. If we were to believe the floor plans, then it was the birthright of every American child to have a walk-in closet and compartmentalized private bath by the time they moved out of the nursery.

All these things would be fine if we had unlimited money to buy stuff with and unlimited energy to run that stuff with. But that's not the case, either on a global scale or on a personal scale, as we have all discovered to varying degrees of pain since the Meltdown.

Double-duty (or more) is not a new idea. Ask your grandparents. The "waste not, want not" ethic was central to nearly every culture around the world less than a century ago. Read Benjamin Franklin and it's clear that America was founded by people who valued frugality instead of celebrating consumption.

I've had a recent close encounter with the need for extreme double-duty. I met with Andrés Duany on the Saturday after Hurricane Katrina and we laid out the foundation principles of what

Katrina Cottage VIII interior partitions are built with shelves, not hollow walls

would soon come to be known as the Katrina Cottages. The idea was to help people gain a foothold on their property again by building unusually small cottages that were appropriate to the architectural needs of the region, excellent in design, and deliverable by all major construction methods: site-built, panelized, modular, and manufactured.

I put out a call to the New Urban Guild for Katrina Cottage designs. Andrés, his partner Elizabeth Plater-Zyberk, and the Congress for the New Urbanism orchestrated the largest planning event in human history (the Mississippi Renewal Forum) on the Gulf Coast just six weeks after the hurricane, with nearly 200 planners, architects, and other professionals participating.

Another partition made of shelves in the kitchen

But even before that event, nearly two dozen Katrina Cottages had been designed by Erika Albright, Bill Allison, Bill Dennis, Victor Deupi, Frank Greene, Gary Justiss, Alex Latham, Matt Lister, Tom Low, Eric Moser, Dan Osborne, Julie Sanford, Laura Welsh, and myself. All work was done for free, of course. During the Forum, several more Katrina Cottages were designed, including the little yellow one by Marianne Cu-

*[left] Bed alcove open by day, [right] closed at night. It's an
old idea, like a canopy bed; it allows a very low thermostat
on winter nights because body heat warms the alcove.*

sato that has since received a great deal of press. Since the
Forum, still others have been designed by an expanding circle
of architects and designers.

One of the biggest lessons we learned is that you can't just
shrink a house and expect people to like it. If you take away
size, you've gotta give something else in return. Ask someone
to move into a cottage half the size of their current house, and
they'll likely turn you down. But if the cottage lives twice as
big as its footage, then that may be a different story.

This is an idea I call the Smaller & Smarter Cottage, and
it has other benefits, too. In order to be Smaller & Smarter,
the cottage has to be able to store a lot more stuff per foot
than the bigger house, but the entire floor plan can't be just
one big closet; everything has to be rethought. We even carve
into the walls themselves, leaving no cubic inch unused. Why
shouldn't interior walls be used for shelving, rather than just

wasted? The side-benefit to this is the fact that the storage methods (such as shelving walls) that are visible can be quite attractive, and contribute mightily to the cottage's charm.

There was another problem, too: the first generation of Katrina Cottages didn't expand very well. This is because in a tiny cottage, the exterior walls quickly get taken up with things that are difficult to move, like kitchen cabinets, bathrooms, and closets.

The second generation of Katrina are called Kernel Cottages because, like a seed, they are designed to grow easily in many directions. People can buy a smaller cottage today than

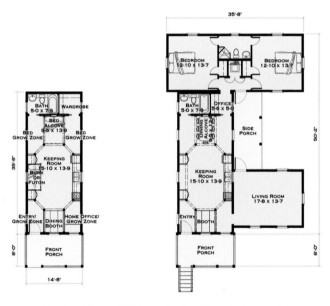

Katrina Cottage VIII was the first Kernel Cottage. It's shown here with one of the many ways it's able to expand from Grow Zones in each corner.

they'll need in the future if the path to expansion is obvious. Before home mortgages, everyone built this way. Thomas Jefferson lived in one of the little garden pavilions on the back side of Monticello for several years while he was building the main house. If Jefferson could do it, why can't we?

Interestingly, one of the things people enjoy most about the character of pre-mortgage houses is the story they tell in the incremental way they have grown from one generation to the next. But it wasn't designed that way from the beginning, as we might suppose today. Rather, it's the character that emerged from many hands working over time.

Beyond the obvious savings in building materials, there's a huge, three-pronged sustainability bonus that comes from building much smaller to begin with, then adding on later: First, because the square footage is a lot less, it costs much

less to condition. Second, because rooms in tiny cottages are likely to have windows on both sides, they cross-ventilate wonderfully in summer, and also daylight beautifully. This saves even more in conditioning expense. Finally, if the designer really does their job and the cottage lives much larger than its footage, people might just discover that they don't need to add such a big addition when it comes time to expand.

5 ~ *the* Source *of* Stuff

This one seems so elementary that you might think it's an item we don't even need to talk about. The further something has to travel while it's being made and sold, the more energy it usually consumes. And common sense tells us that we should be saving energy. So the most sustainable source of stuff should therefore be nearby, right?

Our recent track record, however, says that we have other priorities. Try this test: Turn your head and look around the room. Most of the things you're looking at have traveled thousands of miles to get to you, from the places where the resources were extracted from the earth, to the places where the parts were made, to the factory where the whole thing was assembled, to the warehouse where it was stored, to the shop where you bought it.

Common sense tells us that we're not being green if nearly everything we touch has thousands of Embodied Miles. Some complex things like cars may actually have more Embodied Miles than it takes to go all the way around the world.

I read recently, for example, about a particular Japanese car. Or at least the corporate offices were located in Japan. Materials were extracted in mines around the world. Many of the parts were made in Japan, but were shipped to a factory in the United States for assembly. Finally, some of those cars were shipped back to Japan and other Asian nations to be sold.

In recent years, Everyday Low Prices have been the most important things in commerce. We've voted with our wallets, and Everyday Low Prices are more important to us than the countless small hometown businesses we've lost because they weren't quite so cheap. Everyday Low Prices are more important to us than the millions of jobs that got offshored because we wouldn't work for so much less. Nobody wants to waste money when they're buying toilet paper, even if we're wasting towns and wasting our fellow-citizens' jobs to do it.

But because we don't want to waste money, this may just be one of the only items in this chapter that takes care of itself because as fuel costs rise, as they must certainly do as millions more cars get on the road every year in China and India alone, and as oil supplies dwindle, it's obvious that the cost of shipping stuff around the world can't be sustained.

Sustainable things are things which we can keep going in a healthy way long into an uncertain future. There are many things we don't know about an uncertain future, especially including what the cost of transportation will be, so the only certain sources of stuff in an uncertain future will be those that are nearby. And it's not just the cost of transportation. The world has painfully seen recently how wars can start over resources like oil.

One thing we must do if we want to keep things going in a healthy way is to quit throwing so much stuff away. The Story of Stuff (www.storyofstuff.org) tells an incisive tale of our consuming ways in recent decades. The Story of Stuff deals mainly with consumer goods, but we throw other things away, too... like buildings... even ones as large as the factories in the "Rust Belt" of Northern states abandoned by industry.

But that's not all... if we want to keep things going in a healthy way, then our sources need to be close enough that we can keep an eye on them. Making things in distant lands means that we can't see the horrible conditions people (including children) must endure in the sweatshops, but that's only the beginning. Making things overseas also means that we can't see how bad the environment is being trashed to make our stuff until the effects go global.

How close is close enough? That depends mainly on two things: the weight of the item versus its value and the complexity of the item that's being made. The heavier stuff is, the closer the source should be to where it's used because heavier stuff requires more energy to ship than lighter stuff. Long before the gasoline engine, people shipped spices from one continent to another because the spices were so light enough and valuable enough that a chain of camels could deliver a lot of value on each trip to the traders that owned them. Bricks, on the other hand, were often made from clay dug up in the back yard. That may be a bit extreme today, but you get the picture.

Another factor is the complexity of the item. For instance, it's possible to have a cabinet shop on every corner of a town center, but it's not possible to do the same with a car factory. That's because while the cost of setting up and equipping a simple cabinet shop might be less than the cost of a car, the cost of a car factory is hun-dreds of millions of dollars. So more complex things must be made more centrally and shipped further in order to eventually repay their invest-ment... just not as far as we've been shipping them recently. It's not yet apparent how far is too far, but the best rule is: the closer the better. The best policy would be to live with-in the same region as most of our sources of stuff. Kind of like living within our means.

4 ~ *the* EXPANDED COMFORT RANGE

The human comfort range has shrunk to its smallest size in human history over the past half-century. Our ancestors had a comfort range of probably 30 degrees Fahrenheit. Near 90 degrees, they might cool themselves with a hand-held fan. Near 60 degrees, they would put on an extra layer of clothes. Today, however, there are "thermostat wars" all over the US over 2 degrees. Don't laugh… you likely have participated in some of them at some point yourself. And Jimmy Carter lost his re-election campaign in part because he famously asked Americans to wear sweaters and cut the thermostat down in winter to help with the energy crisis of that day. The sweater therefore became the only article of clothing to ever play a role in ending an American presidency.

Ask any mechanical engineer to describe the impact of a 30-degree comfort range versus a 2-degree comfort range. She will tell you that a 2-degree comfort range requires the conditioning equipment to run basically all the time, because outdoor temperatures are almost never within that 2-degree range. And if the equipment is going to be running almost all the time, why even have windows that are operable? So

they seal up the buildings where you can't ever open a window to catch a breeze.

A 30-degree range, on the other hand, means that there are several months per year when the air outside is within the comfort range at least part of the day. So if the building is designed cleverly enough, it can condition itself for most of the year in many places, requiring mechanical conditioning only in more extreme weather.

How do we expand the human comfort range again, getting it back close to where it has been for almost all of recorded human history? Carter's approach of telling us what we ought to do is no more likely to work now than it did then, as discussed earlier in *7 ~ the Fate of Ought-To* in Part One. People rarely do what they ought to do, and resent being told what they ought to do. But they often do what they want to do. So what's the most effective way of assuring that people want to expand their comfort range?

The best known way is to entice them to go outdoors. As people spend more time outdoors, they become more acclimated to the local environment and need less full-body conditioning when they return indoors.

My own experience provides a good example. I moved to Miami in the fall of 2003. My home on Miami Beach is just

Does this look like a place these people were forced to come to, or is it more likely they were enticed here instead? Not only is it delightful, but health benefits of being outdoors are well-documented.

a few blocks from my office, so I walk. Within a ten-minute walk of my office, I can get to dozens of restaurants, several grocery stores, a hardware store, a drug store, my bank, my doctor, my accountant, and lots more. And it isn't like walking alongside the highway, either... they are highly interesting walks through beautiful places.

Because I walked everywhere, cranking the car only a couple times per week, I quickly became so acclimated to the local environment during that first fall and winter, which is almost always mild in Miami. As springtime turned into summer, I noticed something strange: so long as I was in the shade and could feel a breeze, I was never uncomfortable. That is still true today, almost seven years after moving here: I have never been uncomfortable in Miami so long as there's a breeze in the shade... in a place where the basketball team is named "the Heat," and unaccustomed tourists sweat profusely.

The difference between running the mechanical conditioning equipment all the time and cutting it off several months of the year is so big that it dwarfs any equipment efficiency increases we could hope for in the near future. So which is better: spending lots of money for slightly more efficient equipment that will have a small positive effect on energy use, or spending to create great outdoor public and private realms that will have a large positive effect on energy use, with the added bonus that people get great pleasure out of them?

3 ~ *the* Localized Operations

Sustainability is all but impossible if we have to condition the world, but it becomes easier and easier as we're able to condition smaller pieces of it. Let's look at Waffle House, whose business operates at a distance. Waffle House has the unenviable task of attracting drivers on the distant bridge to come for breakfast. So what do they have to do? Let's take a look.

The first thing they are forced to do is to erect the 200 foot tall sign that probably costs close to $200,000, because travelers at highway speeds will only be on the bridge for a few seconds, and if Waffle House doesn't entice them to exit by then, they've lost their business. Next, because their entire customer base arrives by motor vehicle, they must pave every square yard of their site not occupied

See the tractor-trailer rig on the bridge in the distance? The cab is barely visible, and the driver is microscopic.

by their building for parking to accommodate their customers' cars (the semis must park on the street.) So is there any shadow of doubt why poor Waffle House has such ugly buildings? Of course not! They've completely blown their budget on the sign and the parking lot!

The man in this picture (who happens to be renowned New Urbanist Mike Watkins) arrived on foot to this storefront, and is standing less than ten feet from the sign.

Contrast that with this shop on Nantucket. Because its customers walk up, its sign probably cost much closer to $200 than $200,000. Because this store doesn't have to operate at a wide extent to attract customers, they're able to spend their money on other things... like the high rent in a nice building on Nantucket. Which place would you rather be?

This issue, however, goes far beyond desirable places. Everywhere we look, there are problems that can easily be solved if we're able to do it small, but that become very difficult if we have to do the same thing larger. Consider this extreme example: What if we were able to create clothing that made people comfortable in all but the most ridiculous environments? So if the Boise office is 35°F, no problem... I'm toasty in my enviro-suit. Or if it's 98°F in Orlando, no problem again... I'm completely cool. Conditioning the person rather than the entire building means the cost should be much less. The example is extreme, but it illustrates the point that as the area we have to condition gets smaller, less energy is required.

We operated on this basis for almost all of history. Three Dog Night was a '60's rock band, but long before that, it was a strategy for staying warm... and alive. A one-dog night was

pretty cold, where you let one dog into your bed to sleep on your feet and keep you warm. A two-dog night was colder, and a three-dog night was the coldest night. The canopy bed (like this alcove bed in Katrina Cottage VIII) worked in a similar way... close the curtains, and your body heat (and that of your bed-mate) would keep you toasty even when it was absolutely frigid throughout the rest of the house.

2 ~ *the* SHARING *of* WISDOM

The Sharing of Wisdom and the Involvement of Everyone are so interrelated that we could have lumped them into a single item, but they're so important that it made more sense to tell two stories rather than one so as to cover them more thoroughly. Here's how they fit together: The Sharing of Wisdom is essential if we hope to involve everyone in a sustainable future... and if we *don't* involve everyone, we likely won't *have* a sustainable future. Let's look first at the most common ways that wisdom is already shared. Next, we'll think about how we can do it better.

The three most common current ways of spreading wisdom, from the broadest to the highest, are public education's way, higher education's way, and the specialists' way. Each has strengths and weaknesses. Unfortunately, those weaknesses prevent each of these ways from solving the problems of sustainability on their own. Fortunately, there's a fourth and far more capable way that has been around since the dawn of time; we simply need to rediscover how to tap into it.

Before the internet, the public library was usually the only free educational resource available after graduation from public school.

PUBLIC EDUCATION'S WAY

Public education in most countries spreads wisdom very broadly, but not so high. It begins formally with pre-school, although parents almost always engage in some form of home-based learning before children enter their formal education. Often, it's as simple as story-telling or reading with their children. Next comes elementary and then middle school. Formal public education usually ends with the high school diploma.

Public education after graduation is mostly self-directed. Today, the Internet has firmly replaced both library and bookstore as the primary resource for self-directed learning.

Public education in developed countries intends to reach all children, so it is very broad, normally having the force of law behind it to ensure that all children attend school. And while you can theoretically learn almost anything on the Internet, the fact is that people who have only a public education most often use their education for basic social and economic competencies. In other words, a public education by itself is much more likely to be used to balance a checkbook or text a message to a friend than to find a cure for cancer.

HIGHER EDUCATION'S WAY

Higher education begins with undergraduate education. It can continue with graduate degrees, up to a doctorate degree.

Higher education (undergraduate in particular) can be characterized as years of listening to lectures, working through innumerable problems appropriate to your field of study, showing your work to your professors, getting graded on your work, and eventually getting a degree for all your efforts. Higher education intends to elevate students to levels of wisdom far above those which they usually obtain from public education. But higher education is not very broad. If in doubt, count the number of people in almost any crowd, then ask how many of them have at least one PhD. Normally, it's a very small percentage.

the SPECIALISTS' WAY

A specialist is someone who knows more and more about less and less until they know absolutely everything about only

16" French whisks and 18" French whisks? Who except a chef knows the difference?

one thing. Some disagree, saying they know absolutely everything about nothing at all. Let's use the first, less offensive definition to see how specialists spread wisdom.

Specialists handle a great deal of information on their chosen specialty. This information is more complex than information shared by the general public. In other words, specialists are less likely to discuss things like dogs, cats, and fish with their fellow-specialists, and are more likely to discuss things like Hexadecacarbonylhexarhodium, the Rapid Engineer

Deployable Heavy Operational Repair Squadron Engineers, or the Positron Emission Tomography scanner.

Each of these terms has a long story behind it. Learning everything about the Positron Emission Tomography Scanner, for example, might take years. Because of this, specialists have what amounts to their own private language of technical jargon, each term of which is embedded with lots of meaning that goes unspoken most of the time. These private languages are the necessary by-product of specializing in something.

If you tried to read any of the three terms above out loud, you know that they're each quite a mouthful. The specialists noticed that, too. So in order to save time, they often use acronyms or codes to shorten them. So Hexadecacarbonyl-hexarhodium becomes Rh_6CO_{16}, Rapid Engineer Deployable Heavy Operational Repair Squadron Engineers becomes RED HORSE, and the Positron Emission Tomography scanner becomes the PET scanner. Any slight chance that someone outside a particular specialty might understand specialist jargon goes to zero when the jargon turns into acronyms.

What's the indecipherable acronym for this thing?

This moves the chances of the specialists' knowledge

spreading outside their specialty from "slim" to "none." So what are we left with? We have one system (public education) that spreads low-level information like reading, writing, and 'rithmetic, broadly. At the other end, we have a system that spreads extremely high-level information, but only to a tiny group of specialists, and to make matters worse, it protects that information with an indecipherable secret language known only to members of the specialty. In the middle, we have a system that spreads mid-level information to a middling degree.

The problem should be clear when we consider the fact that while many of the best minds around the world have been working for years to try to figure out how to live sustainably today, they haven't figured it out yet. So it's reasonable to assume that once they do, it's likely to be some extremely high-level wisdom. But if we're going to achieve sustainability, that information needs to spread broadly. Clearly, none of the primary methods we're currently using are up to the task. We need a system with the best capabilities of all our systems.

NATURE'S WAY

It turns out that there is such a system. And it has been around for a long time. It's nature's way. Consider this: the most complex wisdom humans have ever encountered is the human genetic code. Scientists around the world worked for many years just to document the entire human genome, and they're just now beginning the long process of unlocking what it all means. In all likelihood, the task of unlocking it will still be going on a century from now.

[141]

But stop and think for a moment about how that genetic material spreads. Take humans, for example. As we know, the process begins when two humans are attracted to each other. They mate. They breed. (Not necessarily in that order.) And the genetic material is passed on.

But almost none of the people replicating genetic material are genetic scientists. Nearly all of them, in fact, have only on-the-job training in the replication of genetic material. How is this possible?

Nature's way involves a really nifty trick: nature takes the great wisdom of the genetic code and embeds it in beauty. This lowers the bar unimaginably, so that people only have to consider one another attractive; they don't even need a passing knowledge of genetics in order to pass on some genes.

Looking at the young woman in this picture having lunch

with a friend on the streets of Paris, one might conclude that she has a good chance of passing on her genetic material if she so chooses because she has enough beauty to attract a choice of mates. But if you told her that, she might respond "Yes, but there's so much more to me than just my appearance," and she'd be right. Life is that way, too. There's so much more to life than just the process of passing it on. Architecture can work in a somewhat similar way. Here's how:

Someone might work for years to devise the best possible eave for their region. They might do sun angle or wind speed calculations, and take all sorts of other things into consideration. But if they hope to spread the design of that eave by asking people to work out the same calculations (like higher education asks us to work the problems of our field of study) then it's impossible that the eave would spread. If, however, the designer takes the wisdom they've spent years discovering and embeds that in beauty so that people love that eave, then it can spread all over the region. The people should be aware that the design is good for sun and wind, but they don't have to do the calculations if they can simply say "we love this."

I ~ *the* INVOLVEMENT *of* EVERYONE

Everyone must be involved if we hope to achieve real sustainability which, as discussed at the beginning of this book, means "keeping things going in a healthy way long into an uncertain future." From Part One, we saw in *9 ~ the Danger of Wishes* that standards the experts set for other people don't work if the people aren't committed to them. We discussed in *7 ~ the Fate of 'Ought-To'* that people rarely do what someone tells them they ought to do. *5 ~ the Trouble with Consumption* highlights the fact that we all need to change from consuming to conserving, and why that can be a delightful change to make. We looked at *2 ~ the Supply-Side Focus* and discovered that the things that manufacturers can do for us won't be enough. As noted there, *if our behavior doesn't change, our machines can't save us.* And *1 ~ the Two and a Half Billion People* illustrated why business as usual can't possibly get the job done, because the numbers are getting so much bigger so fast.

My own story in *2 ~ the Supply-Side Focus* shows how a change in behavior can be 800% better than the wildest

dream of higher efficiency. So the most effective changes are the changes we can make, not the changes that manufacturers make. We really need to involve everyone. Fortunately, nature's way of sharing wisdom allows us to do exactly that.

But how does it work? Let's look first at how it once worked, and see if that might tell us something about how it can work in our time, so that we can live sustainably today.

the Original Green

We saw at the beginning of this book that originally, before the Thermostat Age, people lived sustainably in most places around the globe. Some cities persisted in the same places with many of the same streets and buildings for hundreds or even thousands of years. But it wasn't because people ar-

bitrarily chose to be green. Rather, if people didn't build sustainably, they would have frozen to death in the winter, died of heat strokes by summer, starved to death, died of terrible diseases, or other bad things would have happened to them. Sustainability wasn't a casual choice; it was survival.

This is the Original Green: a system of collecting, holding, and distributing the wisdom of sustainability. It is the sustainability that all our ancestors knew by heart, and it

was serious business to them, not just marketing fluff. The Original Green is the only delivery vehicle for sustainability that has ever been proven at a large scale over time, and it has worked since the dawn of human history. We are living evidence of this: had it not worked long and broad, we would not be here today. But we are here... and need to move forward. We can't go back in time, nor would we want to. Contemporary life has many advantages. I believe we can weave them into a sustainable future based on Original Green principles.

LIVING TRADITIONS

Wisdom sitting on a shelf does very little good. Like data stored on a hard drive, it's worthless without an operating system. What was the operating system of the Original Green that spread the high-level wisdom of sustainability so broadly that it reached everyone in a culture?

A Fossil

The mechanism capable of doing this is no mystery: it's something we call a "tradition," and it's been around throughout human history. Recently, however, traditions have fallen upon hard times. Once revered as the best carriers of information across the generations, traditions have more recently been reviled, especially over the past century or so, as impediments to progress, especially in architecture and the arts. And so we discarded our traditions, one by one, to the point that we now misunderstand the entire idea. Mention the word "tradition" in architectural circles, and you'll find that people often equate it with "history" and "obsolete."

Here's the problem: because much of architecture and the arts have discarded tradition as a way of storing and sharing information, the only traditions they're familiar with are the historical traditions that were once alive, but are now dead. So it's easy to see how they could equate traditions with history, and with obsolescence.

A Living Creature

Living traditions, however, bear about as much resemblance to dead traditions as living creatures to do to a fossil. They might both have the same shape, but the living creature is alive, whereas the fossil is not. We can copy the form of a fossil, but that doesn't make it a living thing. We can also copy buildings created by historical traditions that were once alive, but that doesn't mean we've created a new living tradition.

Living traditions are the light around the corner.

Matter of fact, most architects don't believe that it's even possible to start a new living tradition today. But because living traditions were the operating system of the Original Green, which is the only way that has ever been proven to deliver sustainability to everyone, it seems worth trying to start them again. But how? It's been a huge mystery. This is something we've never tried to do before, because we've never lost our living traditions of place-making and building-making at the same time before, like we have over the past century.

We don't have to look very far, however, to see that living traditions exist in many other parts of modern life. The blogosphere is one obvious example. It is a vibrant living tradition that began, self-organized, and spread to include hundreds of thousands of bloggers and millions of readers each day, all within the past decade. And it operates firmly within the high-tech realm. Matter of fact, the blogosphere isn't even possible without today's technology.

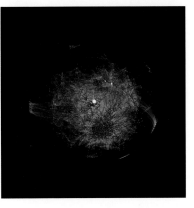

Living traditions, therefore, don't require pre-industrial people and old stuff. Post-industrial humans are clearly capable of living traditions; we just don't have them in architecture right now in most of the developed world.

Blogosphere Network Map
Image source:
http://msa4.wordpress.com

So how do we create new living traditions in architecture? We couldn't even keep them going a century ago; starting them from scratch is a more elusive mystery. Let's take a look at how they died to see if that might give us some hints as to how we might start them again:

*Styles of architecture with a beginning date and an ending
date are like tombstones: they mark the lifespan of something
that once was alive, but now is dead.*

the DEATH *of* TRADITION

Living traditions of places and buildings began to die with
the advent of industrialization, which led to today's hyper-
specialization. In the end, they were buried by a collection
of principles and styles in architecture that we call Modernism. Today, Modernism gets most of the blame (or credit, depending on your position) for destroying tradition because of
its adherents' vigorous and vocal condemnation of tradition.
Modernism, however, merely finished the job; tradition had
been suffering for a long time before Modernism.

Death *by* Specialization

Living traditions capable of spreading the wisdom of sustainability need to operate broadly across a culture, but specialization tends to put people in little silos of their chosen specialty. Prior to industrialization, most people were part specialist and part generalist. They would specialize in an activity that could earn them outside income, but they would build their own buildings, make their own clothes, raise their own food, and make many of their other everyday things.

A few extraordinarily intelligent or talented people could live entirely off their specialty, but most could not afford to buy all the things they needed from the income derived from their specialty. But the great efficiency of industrialization changed all that in at least two ways. By building things much more efficiently, the things became cheaper. The other side of efficiency is that an industrial worker can produce far more stuff in the factory than they could if they were making those same goods or services by hand at home, so they were better off earning money to buy their stuff instead of making it.

At first, the industrial barons kept nearly all of the wealth, and the workers hardly fared better than before. But the rise of the labor movement changed the equation dramatically so that it actually became possible for the first time for the general population to become specialists in one activity, and to trade the income derived from that activity for all of their daily needs of goods and services. By 1925, the specialization of industrialized cultures was nearly complete.

There was, however, a serious unintended consequence: If places and buildings are things we buy from specialists instead of helping to build ourselves, then we have no authority to tell the specialists of places and buildings that what they are providing is not good enough, because they are presumed to know far more about places and buildings than we do.

If you have no authority to tell a specialist that what they  are producing is not good enough (too complex, too narrow, etc.,) and if they are focusing on smaller and smaller aspects of what they are producing as discussed in "the Specialists' Way," then those places and buildings, while they may be produced very efficiently, could not possibly address the complete range of human needs that were addressed when generalists previously made their own places and buildings.

Specialists build great machines, but don't often build great places to live.

Death *by* Licensing

Licensing is where specialization meets architecture. Those who wanted to be architects prior to the 20th century in most places could simply hang out their shingle and begin offering their services. But as the 19th century drew to a close, more jurisdictions began requiring that architects be licensed.

The stated goal was to protect of the public, which makes sense because of changes in the construction industry. Buildings once were often built with relatively crude materials like brick and timber using simple rules of thumb, but modern materials such as steel required more precise design. Most jurisdictions began requiring anything except single-family houses and barns to be designed by architects. Previously, commonplace buildings of many towns were laid out and built by the townspeople. Now, with one stroke of a pen, they were removed to the domain of the architect. This single act removed over half of all buildings from the reach of generalists, and of living traditions, under penalty of law.

DEATH *by* MODERNISM

Modernism arose just as specialization completed its transformation of industrialized cultures. This is no coincidence; Modernism is a classic case of specialization. Its mythology celebrates rare creative geniuses such as Frank Lloyd Wright. An underlying principle, as we saw in Part One's *4 ~ the Achilles Heel of Architecture*, is the necessity of uniqueness for architects who hope to become significant. This requires far more creativity and skill, and the level of discourse is very high. Read the writings of significant architects today and you will find that Modernist discourse is so specialized it's nearly unintelligible to outsiders.

It's not just the high-level creativity and discourse that pits Modernism against living traditions. Modernism, as its very name implies, focuses on all things new, making it essentially an anti-tradition. Things seen as old (like historical traditions) therefore fall easily out of favor amongst most Modernists.

Modernism rode into the 1920s with great optimism, proposing to elevate the lot of the common folk with their great white buildings, finally fulfilling the promise of the industrial revolution to all, not just the industrial barons. This euphoria over the promise of all things new sweeping away the old ossified orders was extremely seductive. Soon, most architects who had any aspirations of greatness converted to Modernism. The list of notable tradi-

tional architects to make the switch is long. Even Wright, then in his 60s, completely re-made himself beginning at Falling Water. The brains had literally been sucked out of traditional architecture in just a few years, like in some alien horror film of a few decades later. It is no surprise that the architecture designed in historical traditional styles in the years that followed was largely schlock.

the Old Mystery *of* New Life

Now that we understand some of the major reasons why living traditions died, it's clear why creating new ones is such a tall order: many of the very underpinnings of the industrial world and its necessary specialization appear to be arrayed against them.

But what of the post-industrial world? Is it possible that some of the new realities of life today such as social media just might be arranged to help bring new traditions to life? We've already discussed the blogosphere coming to life as a new tradition. What would it take to create new living traditions of places and buildings?

The first step has long been a shrouded enigma: how, specifically, do living traditions of places and buildings transmit Original Green wisdom to newcomers, and to the next generation? I was first confronted by this mystery on the day after Thanksgiving, 1980:

the Transmission Device *of* Living Traditions

I was in the middle of architecture school at the time, but home on break at my parents' house. My wife Wanda, my sister Susan, her boyfriend at the time, and I decided that

One of Mooresville's homes

we'd eaten too much turkey the day before, and that we needed to go for a walk. But where? I grew up in a sprawling town
built almost entirely after World War II, and there were very
few places you'd want to walk. So we decided to drive out
to Mooresville and walk there. Mooresville is a little planter's
hamlet, built just a stone's throw from the Tennessee River. It
was founded by simple farmers and tradespeople only three
decades or so after American independence. The town is a
tiny square, only three blocks wide and three blocks deep. We
spent several hours walking every street and photographing
every building on those nine blocks.

Our professors told us that we were going to be the greatest generation of architects ever because we had things like computers that previous generations hadn't had, the contractors building our creations had more powerful tools, and the clients buying our creations had mortgages that were increasingly clever. Yet, I came face to face that day with a startling fact: It's likely that no architect set foot in Mooresville for several decades after its founding, yet those farmers and tradespeople, without computers, power tools, or mortgages, had built a better place than any architect had built from the end of World War II until that day. How could this be? What great wisdom did they possess that allowed simple farmers and tradespeople to build a better place than all the highly trained architects and planners working since World War II?

I finally came to terms with the fact that once people possess

great wisdom like this, those same people can keep using that same wisdom to build in the same way. But that didn't solve the bigger mystery: how did they come to possess that wisdom in the first place, and how were they able to pass it down to the next generation?

Years of travel have revealed that this mystery didn't belong to Mooresville alone. I've found great places like this everywhere I've gone, obviously built mostly by the townspeople, but not by Walt Disney's Imagineers. And most of the medieval quarters of the towns of Europe were built at a time that most people didn't even read or write.

I began calling this mysterious way of transmitting the wisdom of sustainable places the Transmission Device of Living Traditions and hoped that it would be rediscovered in my lifetime. I feared, however, that it might be something mystical, or otherwise unintelligible to post-industrial people. But now, I believe the Transmission Device has been found. The discovery occurred on the evening of July 21, 2004, almost 24 years after the mystery of Mooresville. The New Urban Guild held an architectural charrette, designing homes and other buildings for the town of Lost Rabbit, near Jackson, Mississippi. The charrette concluded that day, and after the celebratory dinner, the design team headed to our B&B, the Millsaps-Buie house. Most of us stood around the parlor, finishing discussions started over dinner.

Late into the conversation, someone asked Milton Grenfell, one of the Mississippi natives on the design team, why

so many of the houses between Jackson and the Coast had "bell-cast eaves," which is a curious term for a roof that turns shallower around the edges. Milton said "*We do this because* moderately steep roofs resist hurricane winds the best, but we need something to break the force of water rushing off the steep roof during our torrential rains..."

I'd been searching for the key to the mystery for many years, but it took a few seconds for Milton's comment to sink in. *"We do this because..." That's it! That's the key!* If every pattern in a language of architecture is framed by "we do this because..." then it opens up the underlying reasons for the architecture, and everyone is allowed to think again! *"We do this because..." is the Transmission Device!* Architecture isn't just some collection of historical styles, but it actually becomes a living thing again! Thinking leads to invention to address new needs, and those inventions free architecture to finally evolve again, as it has always done from the dawn of time until architectural evolution was replaced with the rapid-fire series of revolutions we know as Modernism. And the answer to "we do this because..." shouldn't simply be "it's faster," or "it's cheaper." Those are the specialists' answers, focusing only on one thing. Generalists through the ages take a more holistic view.

Several curious things happen as a result: first, it isn't just about architectural style or fashion anymore, but rather about things with deeper meaning: that which works best for this people, and for this place. Living traditions produce architecture that is simply the best set of ways to build for a particular region's conditions, climate, and culture.

Architecture that allows everyone to think again instead of just following an old set of rules becomes something similar to open-source software because countless people can participate in its development. Many architects aspire to an architecture "of our time." But that which is most intensely "of our time" today is the quickest "outtadate" tomorrow. Contrast that with an architecture that is first of all of here, and also of us: by engaging millions of minds rather than just a few starchitects, a living tradition is capable of producing

the most sustainably modern architecture because it isn't some artistic expression stuck forever in the fashion cycle during which it was created, but instead is being ever updated to meet our needs, and the needs of our place.

There are other benefits: today, many homebuilders persist in building many regrettable details because that's their normal way of building, even though there are far smarter ways of getting the job done.

Until the discovery of the Transmission Device, those of us who were promoting the smarter details could only say "thou shalt do this because I have better taste than you." It was a demeaning proposition, but it was the best we had. But when those discussions were re-framed to begin with "we do this because...", everything changed. Once the builders discover *why* the smarter details are smarter, they're delighted to build using them instead, and actually become advocates for the smarter ways. It's *10 ~ the Things that Work* in practice.

They aren't the only ones. The townspeople often have vague good feelings about certain things they can't quite explain. Maybe it's the way a front porch sits watching the sidewalk, or the way a chimney meets the sky. But in any case, just as soon as someone explains why those elements are the way they are, the townspeople's "warm fuzzies" are transformed into hot-blooded advocacy for the good stuff and they, too, become champions of the smarter and more sustainable ways of building their towns and their homes.

Part Three

What's *the* Plan?

The 8 Foundations of Sustainable Places & Buildings

What happens when you put Original Green theory into practice in our day? It first produces sustainable places, because the carbon footprint of a building is meaningful only if you don't have to drive everywhere in order to inhabit the building. Once the place is sustainable, then buildings that are truly sustainable may be built within it.

Sustainable places are nourishable, accessible, serviceable, and securable. Sustainable buildings are lovable, durable, flexible, and frugal. We'll examine these eight foundations of the

Original Green momentarily, but let's first consider how the whole thing works.

Part Two's *1 ~ the Involvement of Everyone* describes the Original Green as a system of collecting, holding, and distributing the wisdom of sustainability, and how the living tradition is its operating system. This chapter looks at characteristics of the artifacts (places and buildings) the Original Green produces.

Here's another way of visualizing how the Original Green works: because the Original Green is the intelligence behind sustainability, let's consider it as a worker who knows how to build things. A living tradition is the operating system, so let's envision it as a tool. Just as a worker uses a tool to create a product, the Original Green uses a living tradition to produce sustainable places and the sustainable buildings within them.

Being truly green is something that's more than just
skin-deep. The green of this particular home goes much deeper
than just the paint color.

the GREENWASHING *of* AMERICA

Today, almost all manufacturers in America are going through the exercise of proving how their products are the greenest things out there. European companies went through this same exercise a decade ago. If you talk to the steel industry, they'll tell you that steel is the greenest building material...

[167]

and they have lots of marketing materials to prove it. But talk to the wood industry, and they'll have their own reams of brochures to prove their claim. Talk to the concrete industry, and you'll get the same thing. And this is only the construction materials industries. Manufacturers that make everything from cleaning supplies to cars to toilet paper are all doing the same.

But if everything is green, then the term "green" has been reduced to marketing fluff, and is therefore meaningless. As a matter of fact, sustainability that comes out of the marketing department instead of the design department is commonly known as "greenwashing," and is a great disservice to any hopes of real sustainability.

Greenwashing isn't limited to just manufacturers. Any of us could be guilty of greenwashing. How? If we put our

products or services first and try to prove how they lead to sustainability, we're likely greenwashing. Remember, sustainability is the result of changes we make; it comes from the things we do, not just the things we say.

The Original Green therefore takes the opposite approach to greenwashing: it starts with sustainability first and ends up with the things that support it: the foundations of sustainable places, and

*Who could possibly have imagined our modern world
when this place was first built? The deep future is just as
unimaginable to us. How do we prepare for it?*

the foundations of sustainable buildings. How do we "start with sustainability?" We do so by asking the most fundamental sustainability question about both places and buildings: "How do you keep them going in a healthy way long into an uncertain future?"

the SUSTAINABLE PLACES

Let's get to the heart of the matter: What's the first thing we need to keep a place going? Food and drink are the top essentials, because if you can't eat and drink there, you can't live there. If food or drink fail, then the people can't stay very long at all. Places where the food and drink are bountiful and close at hand are Nourishable Places. When Nourishable Places were first proposed several years ago as the top requirement of sustainable places, many people thought this was a crazy idea. Today, however, there is a growing wave of support for the idea, and agricultural urbanism has become the next cool thing in the New Urbanism and beyond.

What's next? Fuel. The only thing we know for sure is that it's going up. As we saw in Part One's *1 ~ the Two and a Half Billion People*, there's about to be 2.5 billion more people about to tax our dwindling supply of gas. How far up will it go? That's anybody's guess. But with each upward move past a certain point, fewer and fewer people will be able to afford to drive. The only certain thing is that we'll still be able to get around by the self-propelled ways of walking and biking if we stay healthy... and walking and biking are two great ways of staying healthy!

What about the other choices? The bigger the vehicle, the more potential riders there are to share the cost of fuel, making light rail, subways, and buses pretty good bets, although still less certain than walking and biking in a future of higher fuel costs. Least certain of all is how long we'll be able to afford to drive ourselves and our goods around as prices rise. That leads us to the second foundation of sustainable places: Accessible Places are those that are accessible by walking and biking. Having access to various forms of transit increases their sustainability.

Walking or biking is great, but if the only reason we walk or bike is for exercise, then that's not so useful. We need to be able to go to meaningful places, like to work and to places where we can get all the basic services of life, which makes those places Serviceable Places. That's where the stage is set for people to be able to make a living where they're living... either within their own homes, within their own neighborhoods, or within adjacent neighborhoods, if they choose to.

What is the final characteristic that might prevent a place from being sustained long into an uncertain future? How safe does the place feel? Cities all over America nearly emptied out in the late 1960s and 1970s because they became scary

places to live. Too much fear for our own safety, that of our families, and the security of our belongings will eventually cause those who can afford it to leave their homes and move elsewhere... not nearly so fast as if you can't eat there, can't get around there, or can't get your basic services there... but eventually, the place will be mostly deserted. A Securable Place is one that is designed in such a manner that it can adjust its configuration slightly to be more secure at those inevitable but hopefully brief periods in the future when things aren't as safe as they are today.

OTHER ELEMENTS *of* SUSTAINABLE PLACES

What might be some other sustainability factors? A place isn't sustainable without economic activity, but a Serviceable Place sets the stage for all sorts of commerce, plus the act of providing food and drink in a Nourishing Place fosters economic activity. A place isn't sustainable without social networks, but Accessible Places provide a deep web of physical connections, and Serviceable Places provide reasons for people to get out into that web, while Securable Places give them the assurances necessary to do so. There are several additional human components to sustainable places, but this chapter is primarily about the physical artifacts (places and buildings) the Original Green produces, so we will focus here on those physical artifacts and how they can set the stage for the human components to first occur and then flourish.

the NOURISHABLE PLACES

A Nourishable Place is one where you look out onto the plants and onto the waters from which much of your food can come. Why "nourishable"? When the Original Green was first conceived, nobody had come up with a suitable word because most people weren't thinking of food as the most essential element of sustainable places. There are very few places in the US today where you can look out onto the fields and waters from which your food already comes. But using the hopeful term nourish*able* (in the future) instead of nourish*ing* (in the present,) includes places that aren't yet nourishing their people, but could do so in the future.

A Nourishable Place may be highly urban or quite rural, or anywhere in between, incorporating agriculture as large as an employing farm or as small as a window garden into the urbanism. Paris and London once reserved bands of gardens around them to feed them. Towns and villages (think Tuscan hill towns,) because they are smaller, may allow agriculture to snuggle closer around them.

OVERCOMING INDUSTRIAL FOOD CHAIN PROBLEMS

Nourishable Places are able to nestle in closely with the larger scales of agriculture and include it within the fabric of the town only when it is good-neighbor bio-intensive gardening. Mega-scale industrial agriculture such as fields that require crop dusting or industrial hog farms are bad neighbors; it's obvious because nobody wants to live anywhere near them. There are other problems with the

Your produce may start out fresh enough somewhere in another country, but...

industrial food chain. Because it thrives at the largest scales of fields, processing plants, warehousing, and super-center sales, it spreads its tentacles broadly. Today, the ingredients of an average meal in the US travel over 1,500 miles to get to your table, and that number is growing every day. Many of those ingredients actually need a passport to get to your plate.

Why should this matter? Aren't Everyday Low Prices the most important thing about groceries? Maybe not. Think for a moment what you'd feel like after spending three weeks in the back of a truck to get from a farm to your kitchen. You'd be bedraggled, wouldn't you? So are your fruits and vegeta-

... after weeks of this, it's no wonder it needs genetic engineering to look edible!

bles. Matter of fact, agribusiness noticed that they fared so badly that they decided to re-make them. So they genetically engineered them to be more durable during all that travel. But when you shop, would you prefer a durable tomato or one that is fresh and juicy? Because this manipulation of our food has taken place over a decade or two, the changes have been slow enough that we haven't really noticed. But try this test: buy that durable tomato down at the super-center, then find one of your neighbors who is still raising heirloom tomatoes, and see if they'll give you one. Take them home, slice them open, and have a taste. The difference will likely be shocking.

MAKING GENETIC ENGINEERING UNNECESSARY

And it's not just an issue of taste. The genetic engineering required to make a durable tomato has the side-effect of creating a tomato that's much less nourishing. So the durable tomato not only tastes like a mere shadow of the natural tomato, but it's not nearly as good for you, either. And what other unintended side-effects might be lurking underneath all that genetic engineering? Let's not even go there... just eat the real thing and you don't need to worry about it. And just remember that the natural home of real food is a Nourish-

ing Place, while the industrial food chain is continually creating stuff that is increasingly unnatural. So much so that noted author Michael Pollan calls them "food-like substances." Do you think there's really much chicken in those "chicken nuggets"?

CHARACTERISTICS *of* GOOD-NEIGHBOR AGRICULTURE

Nourishable Places foster agriculture with the following characteristics: Gardens are opportunistic, occurring wherever there is available earth. It is possible to use edible annuals, edible perennials, and edible trees as a part of edible landscaping that is also beautiful. The Tuscan landscape is purely agricultural, but is some of the most famously beautiful land in the world. Gardens are slope-adaptable, terracing hillsides where they climb steeply. Gardens often incorporate multiple layers, with both tall plants and short plants growing in the same place. They also incorporate raised beds rather than rows, with narrow footpaths in between, so that a person on the footpath can reach to the center of the bed.

Increasing Agricultural Efficiency

All of these things help make good-neighbor agriculture very acre-efficient. It's not nearly so efficient in man-hours as industrial agriculture if only count the guy on the tractor, but consider the full industrial food chain which includes millions of "invisible farmers" in corporate headquarters of agribusiness corporations, in processing plants, and on the highways

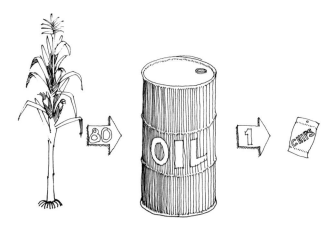

hauling countless gallons of fuel and foodstuffs. Speaking of fuel, the industrial food chain is enormously calorie-inefficient. Michael Pollan reports that if you count the crop plus all of the oil that it takes to cultivate it, harvest it, process it, deliver it, and sell it, we use up approximately 80 calories of crops and fuel to deliver one calorie of food to the table!

There's one more efficiency aspect to consider: the difference in acre-efficiency. The industrial food chain's efficiency is somewhere between 1 and 3 acres per person fed, depending on the growing season and the quality of the land. Good-neighbor agriculture, however, can feed upwards of 20 people per acre in most places because it is far more intensive. But this stunning difference isn't just en-

tertaining. Rather, it might actually play into our survival. The carrying capacity of the world is the number of people the world can support. Nobody knows what that number is, but with 6 billion people alive today on the way to 9 billion by mid-century, it's increasingly likely that we may find that limit within the lifetimes of many of us. But do we really want to go there? What's the alternative?

Clearly, we must begin to stabilize population growth some-how, because everything fails at some point soon (see page 71) if world population continues to accelerate. But it's also clear that good-neighbor agriculture feeding 20 or more people per acre may be our best hope of extending our window of opportunity. In the end, Nourishable Places may not only make a place more sustainable, but they may make our entire planet more sustainable as well.

It's far beyond the scope of this book to solve the problem of population stability, but consider this: it once took lots of work but little resources to live. Because of our cleverness, it now takes little work but lots of resources... leading to far higher population. It will take wisdom to put them in balance and stabilize humanity.

the ACCESSIBLE PLACES

An Accessible Place is one that is accessible by a variety of ways, especially including the self-propelled ways of walking and biking. Larger employment centers require larger populations of potential employees, so fewer people will be able to make a living where they're living in a city. The necessity of transit therefore increases with city size. Without it, cities

A great place to walk is often a great place to run, too.

choke with traffic as they grow, no matter how many extra lanes they build.

Self-propelled transportation choices are preferred above those that are driven by engines, because transportation choice isn't just about using less fuel, but includes the option of using no fuel at all. The benefits of walking and biking go beyond

Classic case of Automotive Poverty: Think how much it would benefit this family if they didn't need cars and could spend that $50,000/year on other things!

saving fuel, however, as they are the only modes of transportation that actually make you healthier. Because they foster walking and biking as major transportation choices, Accessible Places almost always foster other human fitness activities.

Accessible Places don't just foster physical wellness; they also contribute to financial health. The average cost of owning and maintaining a car varies according to location between approximately $7,000 and $10,000 per year. Living in sprawl requires everyone of driving age to own a car if they want to be economically viable. This creates a condition known as Automotive Poverty because compulsory car ownership impoverishes countless families by taking money that might be spent on groceries, clothes, or other necessities out of their pockets to pay for their cars.

Car ownership in Accessible Places, however, is often a choice instead of a necessity. As noted in Part One's *2 ~ the Supply-Side Focus,* Wanda and I got rid of one of our cars when we moved to Miami Beach, and we often go for days without driving the one we kept. Our oldest son just graduated from culinary school and moved to South Beach, too, and he gets around just fine without a car. So the three of us have gone from three cars to one purely because we now live in an Accessible Place, enriching us by about $20,000 per year that we can now choose to save or spend on other things.

Automotive Poverty isn't just financial. Countless millions of Americans are trapped each day, forced to spend more quality time with their steering wheels than with their families. A one-hour commute each way translates into over 500 lost hours per year, and that's if you don't work weekends. But that's only the beginning, because sprawl doesn't just require you to drive to work;

Our single remaining car… it's the Smart that's parked sideways.

it makes you drive everywhere. The real time lost is likely half again as much, or maybe more. You could figure out how much money all that lost time might be worth, but the real cost is more than money. Think what you'd do with all that time if you had the choice: sure, you might work more, but you also might spend more time with your family. Or maybe you'd pursue that new venture you've been dreaming of, but never have time to do anything about. Moving to an Accessible Place might be one of the best changes you ever made. It certainly was for me and for my family.

What actually determines whether a place is an Accessible Place or not? Some of the factors are external, like whether there are transit links. But most of it is internal, or happens around the edges of the neighborhood where the shops and

workplaces are. Walkability isn't just determined by how safe it is to walk, but also whether there's anything meaningful to walk to. If the only thing you can do is walk in loops around a subdivision for exercise, then it's not a walkable place. Walkability is more than just going around and around like a hamster on a wheel. Real walkability happens when you can walk out of one door and into another, like walking to the corner store, or even walking to work, like I do.

Other important walkability factors occur at the scale of the street and the sidewalk. Simply building sidewalks isn't enough. The character of the walking experience is paramount. Sidewalks located between a busy street and a parking lot will almost never see a pedestrian unless someone has a flat tire. Tree-shaded sidewalks protected by on-street parking, on the other hand, are much more likely to be used regularly.

The condition on the private side of the sidewalk is also very important. This is where most of the interest lies. The ability to entertain pedestrians with constantly-changing views is the largest component of Pedestrian Propulsion, which is the ability of the place to propel pedestrians along their way. Places like central Rome, Paris, or London have sky-high Pedestrian Propulsion on most of their streets. There, you can

*These two women were meeting for the first time as this
photograph was taken, due in large part to proper design of
the Private Frontage.*

walk for miles. But places like "power centers" (all big stores)
have pedestrian experiences so bad that most people get in
their cars and drive between the Old Navy and the Barnes &
Noble. Those places actually have Pedestrian Propulsion rat-
ings of less than zero, so in those cases, we call it Pedestrian
Impedance because it makes you want to stop walking.

[186]

The private side of the sidewalk, known as the "private front-age" in New Urbanist circles, has another important attribute. Properly designed, it can actually help people meet and get acquainted, which is what you see happening in the photograph on the opposite page. Until recently, people thought that the design of porches, fences, galleries, and arcades was an art form. Now, we know that it's more of a science, where vertical and horizontal distances between the front porch edge and the back edge of the sidewalk are crucial, as are the character of the frontage hedge, fence, or wall and the porch or gallery rail. Mess these up, and unplanned conversations will seldom if ever occur. But get them right, and you've set the stage for something that's almost miraculous: people that didn't previously know each other have unplanned conversations. Those conversations lead to acquaintances, and those acquaintances

(this sounds trite, but it's true) actually result in people acting like neighbors again. And places where your fellow-inhabitants are your neighbors for several blocks around are the places where you're most drawn to walk and bike. It's no stretch to say that walkability puts the "neighbor" back in "neighborhood."

the SERVICEABLE PLACES

Serviceable Places are those where the basic services of life are within walking distance in your neighborhood, so that driving is a choice, not a necessary act of survival. They also have places where the people offering you those services can afford to live nearby. Serviceable Places finally give us the choice of detaching ourselves from the highway, that umbilical cord of the industrial era, so that we can once again make a living where we're living if we want to.

Just a decade ago, that would have seemed like an impossible dream for most people because their workplaces were immovable. Today, however, an increasing number of corporate employees are working from home, and their companies, by most reports, seem pleased with the situation. Homes in Serviceable Places lead the way in providing home workplaces. Some let you work within your home, in a workshop behind your home, in a storefront in front of your home, or in an office beside your home. Others allow you to live above the shop, in respected Main Street fashion.

Places where you can live and work are also great for another reason. Post-Meltdown layoffs have created an unprecedented flood of people needing to make a living some other way, and many are choosing to open their own businesses since the prospects of getting a job with another employer are so dim. Trying to rent space for your new business in hard times is terrifying; working from home creates a far stabler foundation for your new venture.

The biggest problem is the fact that working from home is strictly illegal in countless places. New Urbanist developers have fought valiantly to get the home workplace approved in their developments. They call it the "live-work unit." Other people, however, have long assumed that when a business moves into a neighborhood, decline isn't far behind, so they've vigorously opposed any mixing of residential and commercial uses.

The New Urbanism has a long track record of mixed use that clearly shows that when the character of the shop is correct, real estate values actually increase. Put another way, while a convenience store down the block would definitely destroy property values for everyone nearby, a general store on the corner built in a way respectful of the neighborhood's architecture would clearly have the opposite effect. The key isn't so much what the building is used for (except for really noxious uses,) but whether or not it's designed as a good neighbor.

Equally important is the scale of the building. It's impossible for a modern auto assembly plant, no matter how beautiful the building, to make a good neighbor on the next block. Actually, it wouldn't even *fit* on the next block... it would require many blocks. But scale is a problem with businesses much smaller than a factory: a mega-church or a super-center would all be misfits in most neighborhoods, even though they're several times smaller than the factory.

But isn't scale the secret to efficiency? Haven't we all been told for years that "we're big enough to serve you," implying that businesses any smaller can't serve us? There's a dirty little secret of efficiency of service: it's not the size of the building that matters, but rather the size of the crew. The right question is: "How many people does it take to perform the core task of this business?" If you own a hotel, then the core task is cleaning the rooms, and that task has a crew of one. Each maid can clean about 8 rooms per day. This means that a bed & breakfast with 8 rooms requires one person to clean the rooms, whereas a 40 room hotel requires 5... and both will be similarly efficient at getting the job done. But an inn of 13 rooms is too big for one person, and will be notably less efficient with two people cleaning the rooms, even though it's larger than the B&B. So the benchmark we should be interested

in if we want to create Serviceable Places is the Single-Crew Workplace: what does a given business look like when it contains just a single crew working at optimum efficiency? Chances are, it will look like a good neighbor building in your Serviceable Place.

Interestingly, good neighbors in Serviceable Places come in many varieties. American developers, however, have been terrified of introducing them to each other in suburban sprawl. There, the subdivisions are finely stratified by income level, so that your neighbors are just like you. The developers apparently don't mind that this is the best known recipe for boredom. They assume, incorrectly, that most people are horrified to meet someone not exactly like them.

Meanwhile, people living in the New Urbanist places or old neighborhoods built or revitalized recently are continually and pleasantly surprised to turn a corner and run into some of their interesting neighbors that aren't just like them. Maybe it's the policeman that protects them, or one of the fire-fighters. Or maybe the schoolteacher that teaches their children, or the barista who serves up the cappuccino in the morning, or that young chef whose star has recently been rising down at the corner grill. Or maybe it's one of their own kids. Yeah, that's right... Serviceable Places also include Next-Genera-

tion Houses where your kids can afford to live when they graduate from college. Maybe all these people can't afford to live right around the corner from you, but if they can live somewhere in your neighborhood or in nearby neighborhoods, their daily commute can be a walk or a bike ride if they choose, rather than the 50 mile drive many of them currently have to endure in many increasingly unaffordable places across the country.

the SECURABLE PLACES

   A Securable Place is one that can be physically adjusted in the future so that there is not undue fear for your own safety, that of your family, or the security of your belongings. A place that is "secur*able*" rather than "secure" is one that sets the stage for physical security elements to be installed later in those hopefully brief moments in the future when things aren't as safe. They may never be needed, but if they are, it could make all the difference between a place that can be sustained through difficult years and one that nearly empties out, like cities all over the US did during those painfully anti-urban years from the late 1960s through the beginning of the 1980s.

This is a very difficult conversation to have, because so much emotion it pent up in so many of us because of the scars left behind by those years. Those who left are scarred because they had to uproot their families from their homes and move somewhere unfamiliar because their neighborhoods had become too frightening. Those who stayed behind were scarred, too, from watching their once-vibrant neighborhoods turn into veritable ghost towns... or worse. So there's no doubt it's a difficult conversation, but it's one we must have if we don't want to repeat those mistakes in the ominous years of some uncertain future.

Interestingly, when most people think of secure places, they think of gated subdivisions, but let's take a closer look: Some problems are obvious, such as the fact that police and fire protection services are slower simply because the emergency responders have to open the gate. Maybe it's only a few seconds' difference, but that could be all the difference in the world if your life hangs in the balance. And what happens when the criminals move in with you? Recent news stories tell of drug dealers moving into gated subdivisions precisely because police response time was slower, giving them more time to conceal the evidence.

But there are more insidious side-effects. They all begin with the fact that gated subdivisions as we know them are all too small to have a viable mix of uses. Try to put a store within them, and it will die because the only possible customers are the people that live within the gates, and there simply aren't enough of them to make businesses viable. This single fact starts an entire avalanche of unintended consequences.

If the gated subdivision can't support retail or services other than the clubhouse, that means that you must drive outside the gates for everything else. Auto-dominated retail has a character that is extremely unfriendly to pedestrians. It's where you

buy "drive-through drugs" rather than walking to the corner pharmacy. It's where you drive to the gym so you can walk on the treadmill. It's where your snacks, drinks, and news come from vending machines, not from a little sidewalk cafe... because there is no sidewalk. There's no reason to create a good pedestrian experience between gated subdivisions and auto-dominated retail centers because why would you walk

there if it's a horrible place to walk when you get there? To confirm this, sit outside a gated subdivision all day and count the number of people that walk to the strip center. Chances are, your count will be precisely zero.

Places where the basic services of life are not within walking distance can't be Serviceable Places. Unwalkable places cannot be Accessible Places, either, because they're missing the most important means of access: walking. So gated subdivisions can't be sustainable places. If you doubt this, watch what happens in coming decades as they begin to age.

So if the gated subdivision isn't a model for Securable Places, then what is? First, do all normal things to make a safer place, like designing so that there are more "eyes on the street," as Jane Jacobs said. There are two primary candidates for making a place securable in the future. The first and smallest-scale model is the securable block. Here, the street frontages of the buildings are closely aligned, and could be connected more firmly by frontage walls if future conditions warrant. Each end of the alley or mews court could be gated if necessary, so that only the residents of that block (which are the people you know the best) have access to the interior of the block, but the streets are open for all, so it's still an Accessible Place. European cities were built using this pattern for centuries.

The second and oldest model is the town that can be gated if necessary. These are completely different from gated sub-divisions because they're large enough to enclose the entire town, so they can be Accessible and Serviceable. Medieval towns all over Europe followed this form, and they're some of the most delightful places to walk in the world. They're

also thickly populated with shops, workplaces, and inns, providing a vibrant environment where there are many things to walk to. Because there's a clear edge of the town, secured on the inside but unsecured on the outside, real estate values drop sharply at the wall, leaving land outside inexpensive enough to be used for agriculture. This means these towns can easily become Nourishable Places, too.

the SUSTAINABLE BUILDINGS

What's the first thing we must do to a building to assure that it lasts long into an uncertain future? Our track record makes it clear that, after an inexplicable period of national amnesia culminating with the destruction of New York's Penn Station, we preserve what we love, and discard what we don't. Nothing condemns a building to the wrecking ball faster and with more certainty than if it is unlovable. Sustainable buildings must therefore first be lovable. What's next? If a building is lovable enough to be preserved, then it needs to be durable enough to endure long into an uncertain future. Durability, which should not be confused with strength, is a function of the materials we choose and also how we use them.

If a building is both lovable and durable, then it is likely to

far outlast its initial intended use. This means that it needs to be flexible enough to be used for many things over the centuries, some of which were not even dreamed of at the time the building was first designed and constructed.

Buildings that are lovable, durable, and flexible also need to be frugal. Few things are worse than a lovable, durable energy hog because you can't get rid of them... the townspeople won't let you!

the Lovable Buildings

If a building cannot be loved, it will not last. Any serious conversation about sustainable buildings must begin with the issue of Lovability. If a building cannot be loved by those using and visiting it, then it is likely to be demolished and carted off to the landfill in only a generation or two, at which point its carbon footprint is meaningless. All of the embodied en-

ergy of its materials is lost (if they are not recycled.) And all future energy savings are lost, too. Buildings continue to be demolished for no other reason except that they cannot be loved. Even an architectural landmark as celebrated as the Boston City Hall is in danger of this fate because only an architect could love it. It is not rational to consider a building to be sustainable when its parts reach a landfill in a generation or two.

RECYCLE *or* PRESERVE?

The popular green community is now advocating that every building should have a plan for its eventual demolition and recycling. At first, this seems like an honorable goal. But in reality, it is an admission of the inability to build in a lovable fashion. Our ancestors once built for the ages, and the best of their buildings could last for a thousand years or more. Even the everyday buildings lining every street regularly lasted for centuries. And they lasted because they could be loved. So the real question should be: Is it better to throw something away and then hire someone to recycle it, or rather to preserve it so that it doesn't need to be thrown away? The answer should be obvious: it's far more sustainable not to throw things away... including buildings.

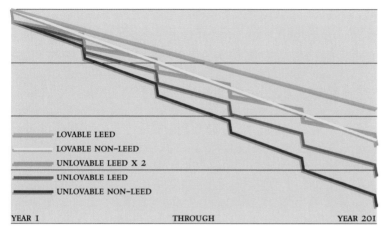

LOVABLE LEED
LOVABLE NON-LEED
UNLOVABLE LEED X 2
UNLOVABLE LEED
UNLOVABLE NON-LEED

YEAR I — THROUGH — YEAR 20I

PRESERVATION *vs.* LEED

Let's take a closer look at preservation and sustainability. This chart shows five types of buildings charted over 200 years. The lines all go downward because each building type consumes more energy than it makes. The three unlovable types each have a sharp step down every 40 years. These sharp steps are the energy required to demolish and rebuild the buildings plus the embodied energy of the building materials. Some unlovable buildings like big-box super-centers are demolished in as little as 10 years, whereas tract houses are more likely to last 50-75 years, so 40 is an approximate average lifespan of all unlovable building types.

The difference between the Unlovable Non-LEED line and the Unlovable LEED line is the average efficiency increase of all LEED buildings (certified, Silver, Gold, & Platinum) according to the US Green Building Council, which founded the LEED green building standard. The Lovable LEED x 2 line is for a building twice as good. Lovable Non-LEED is an historic building that has demonstrated that it's lovable by being there for a long time already. Its line shows what happens if you do nothing but change the filters and do the other normal stuff to keep it in good operating condition.

Shockingly, as you can see on the chart, historic buildings perform as well as unlovable buildings that are twice as good as the current LEED standard! The best condition, of course, is represented by the Lovable LEED line, which is an historic building that has been retrofitted with better equipment so that it meets the LEED standard. But in any case, preserving a lovable building is better than throwing it away and replacing it with something not so lovable, even if the building you're replacing it with has high energy efficiency. Preservation should be considered the everyday acts of sustainability because sustainability isn't likely if we keep throwing stuff away. Sustainability, which means "keeping things going in a healthy way long into an uncertain future," begins with "keeping things," after all.

How is it that we forgot this basic green fact? I believe we began to let it slip away in the 1960s and 1970s, during the last Green Revolution, and the fact that we let it get away was an important part of the way that revolution ended.

How *the* First Green Revolution *was* Lost

The images on both of these pages show devices that create heat. The device on the left is a hot water solar collector; the one on the right heats the air. Both of them are engineered to work properly, but only one of them is designed to be lovable. As a result, we can easily imagine the chimney existing several centuries into the future. Not so for the collector.

Rooftop solar collectors like the one on the left were installed by the millions in the 1970s. Just a decade later, they were ripped off by the millions and carted off to the nearest landfills. People said "I don't care if it *is* saving me money, get that *hideous thing* off my roof; *I won't tolerate it any longer!*"

Because the artifacts of that Green Revolution were conceived only as engineering, rather than engineering *plus*

design, the people turned against the revolution, and an entire generation of time was lost.

That *could* happen to us. It doesn't *have* to happen to us. But it *could*, if we don't design our green stuff to be lovable if it's visible. Because we don't have another generation of time to waste, we really need to get busy now designing stuff rather than just engineering it. Our children will thank us.

WHAT MAKES THINGS LOVABLE?

"Love" is a term that includes a wide range of favorable emotions, from a soft resonance so gentle it can often be missed to passion so strong that people are occasionally willing to die for it. Because this chapter is about the artifacts of the Original Green, we'll limit this discussion to the objects we love and how we love them. It should be noted that people are sometimes known to die for ideals, and also for other people, but it's difficult to recall the last sane person who has died for an object. Because this chapter is about objects (places and buildings,) we'll focus on love which isn't to die for.

Resonance is both the lowest and most common form of love we'll examine. How should we arrange the things with which we resonate? It seems that there are three general categories: things that reflect us, things that delight us, and things that put us in harmony with something larger than us. Things that reflect us are drawn from us. Things that delight us are given to us. Things that put us in harmony are the things that balance us.

i ~ Things *that* Reflect Us

Things can reflect us in several ways. They can reflect our physical form or they can reflect our larger culture. Things that reflect our physical form can reflect the shapes of our bodies, the arrangement of our parts (both vertically and horizontally) or they can reflect our bodies' proportions. Cultural reflections can occur anywhere from the scale of a tribe to the scale of a nation or even a continent.

REFLECTING *the* HUMAN FORM

Beginning with the human form, if we focus on what it means to be human rather than just what is popular in the current fashion cycle, then it is clear that some things have resonated with humans through the ages. These include objects that reflect the 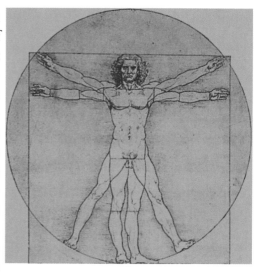 human body's shape, arrangement, and proportions. For example, we have a head, a body, and feet. Shapes that reflect our vertical arrangement have a top, a middle, and a bottom. Things as large as a building or as small as a baseboard do this.

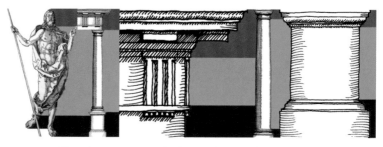

Vertical arrangement: The human form has head, body, and feet. The classical order has top, middle, and base also, from the scale of the whole to the scale of the smallest part.

From side to side, we are arranged symmetrically (at least on the outside) with a pair of arms, a pair of legs, a pair of eyes, etc. Our symmetry can be very relaxed, like when a kid is sprawled out on a couch, or may be very rigid, like a soldier standing at attention, but our faces are always pretty much symmetrical. So we have the choice of arranging our limbs either symmetrically or asymmetrically according to the formality of the occasion, but unless we are horribly disfigured in some terrible accident, our face is always arranged symmetrically about our nose. Architecture has traditionally mirrored this arrangement: wings may be more or less symmetrically arranged according to the formality of the building, but the entrance typically mirrors the symmetry of our face in some way. Internally, buildings are often arranged like our internal organs: less symmetrical according to the job each room needs to do.

Humans have long been known to resonate with the shape of the human body and also the shape of the human face. Any kindergarten art class can confirm that this resonance occurs very early in life; children regularly draw pictures of a house that look strikingly like a human face. This is likely easier for kids from more organic cultures where shelters more closely resemble the human form.

Numerous building elements reflect proportions of appropriate parts of the human body. There are many examples; one classic is the proportion of window panes. While they vary in a range similar to the variations in human bodies, they are traditionally vertical, mirroring the proportions of the human faces that look out of a building through them. Doors are often of taller vertical proportions for a utilitarian reason: to allow humans to walk through them. Others are more esoteric. Leonardo da Vinci's Vitruvian Man drawing on page 206 shows the harmony of human and mathematical proportions.

REFLECTING OUR CULTURE

Buildings, their parts, and the towns they're built within can reflect our culture in a number of ways, from the scale of our tribes to the scale of our nation. Artifacts that reflect our culture are often symbolic in some way, carrying embedded

meaning to members of the culture.

Tribal culture includes everything from religions to tribes built around trades, politics, athletic teams, or individual celebrities. Tribal artifacts are often of the smallest physical size, such as this icon of my trade.

Front Porch: Cultural icon of the American South.

Regional culture is often reflected by building parts or utility buildings. Think of the stone towers attached to the buildings of Tuscan hill-towns, the stoops of Brooklyn, or the Southern porches such as the one pictured above.

National or continental culture is reflected more often by entire buildings. Sometimes they are buildings that occur many times, such as Dutch windmills and Oriental pagodas. In other cases, a single iconic building such as the Eiffel Tower, the Taj Mahal, or the Empire State Building can accomplish the same thing.

2 ~ THINGS *that* DELIGHT US

There are several forms of delight that places and buildings can deliver. The most common delight is purely sensual. Places and buildings may also set the stage for "group delight," which occurs as a result of interactions with others. They may also serve as anchors for memories, allowing past pleasures to be revisited for a lifetime. They may serve (especially the buildings) as vehicles of intellectual delight. The last two delights are opposites: one is the sheltering delight, while the other is the challenging delight.

SENSUAL DELIGHT

The most basic of delights delivered by buildings and places work directly on our senses. These are things like the murmuring gurgle of a courtyard fountain on a sweltering afternoon, or the way a Charleston porch catches the sea breeze as spring days give way to summer, or the radiant warmth of coals in the fireplace as crackling flames fade to embers late on an evening that's brittle cold outside. Sensual delight needs

no words; if you doubt this, just look at the cat curled up on the edge of the hearth.

Group Delight

Group delight isn't something a building or place delivers, but rather something that it allows by providing the backdrop upon which interactions between people may occur. The most obvious and ancient purveyors of group delight are stadia and arenas where communities gather to cheer on the hometown favorites, and religious buildings where believers shared a sometimes higher-minded and often other-worldly delight.

Memory Delight

A building can act as a talisman to conjure up memories of long-ago events. Ever notice how you feel you've lost a part of yourself when a building that houses many of your memories is demolished? Before industrial architecture, our buildings did this job well because they were unique. But today, much of our world has been reduced to cells in a matrix. Suite numbers are poor substitutes for memorable buildings.

How can your mind store a memory where everything is almost exactly alike?

INTELLECTUAL DELIGHT

Buildings can create intellectual delight that is quite the opposite of sensual delight, working almost entirely through the mind rather than the raw senses. Because it works by telling a story, or providing hints and clues to one, it requires participants to know some background material. This delight is therefore accessible to you only after you know the underlying story.

SHELTERING DELIGHT

Buildings create sheltering delight in a number of ways. Chief amongst them is the "roof over my head" in both a symbolic and an actual sense. In other words, we need to get out of the weather regularly to stay healthy and to be fully func-

tional, but we also appreciate the image of a sheltering roof and the elements that hold it up. The delight of having a place to rest is closely related. Nurturing delight is a two-way street. Buildings nurture us by providing shelter and a place to thrive. But our nesting instinct is our hardwired need to reciprocate by nurturing our buildings. This is most evident in the way we nurture our gardens, made as they are of living things.

Challenging Delight

Sheltering delight's counterpart is the challenging delight. This pair, taken together, has a strong male-female subplot; mothers are more often the nurturing ones, while fathers are characteristically the most challenging. But what, in particular, is a challenging delight? There are several:

Let's carry the male-female analogy a bit further: While sheltering delights tend to be inward-turning and sometimes even womb-like, challenging delights tend to be thrusting out, or outward-looking. While a view to an inner garden courtyard is a sheltering delight, a window opening to a vibrant street can be a challenging delight.

There is a dark side. Miami, for years beginning with the Mariel boatlift, was very popular with European tourists precisely because there was a chance you might get killed vacationing here. The voodoo places of New Orleans thrive for similar reasons.

In other cases, there's no mortal danger, but rather just the risk of striking out to places and experiences unknown. Seaports, train stations, and airports all fulfill this function in actuality, and should enhance the challenging nature of the experience by fulfilling it symbolically, too.

3 ~ THINGS *that* PUT US *in* HARMONY

Places and buildings can put us in harmony with things larger than ourselves in several ways. They can reflect mathematical proportions that have long been proven harmonious with many things in nature. Buildings can be built in harmony with natural processes of life, and also with laws of nature. They can include symbolic and actual elements from nature. Finally, they can be harmonious with (or appropriate to) the regions of the world in which they are located.

Mathematical Harmony

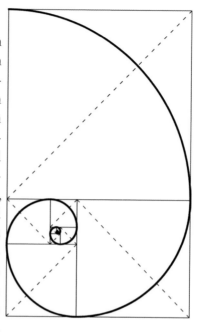

Humans, as discussed in "Reflecting the Human Form," resonate with proportions found in the human body. They also resonate with a set of mathematical proportions that are both rational (1:1, 4:3, 3:2, etc.) and irrational (the square root of 2, the Golden Mean (illustrated here,) etc.) These proportions are found pervasively in nature, from the shape of a nautilus shell to a ram's horn to microscopic structures. Some of them spell out the harmonies of the musical scale, prompting Johann Wolfgang von Goethe to observe that architecture that respects these proportions is "frozen music."

Harmony *with* Natural Processes

Janine Benyus popularized the idea of biomimicry beginning in the late 1990s. It's an examination of ways we can use nature's processes to improve our own, such as looking at how spiderwebs can inform structures we build. Recently, a number of architects have adopted the idea, but only superficially. They might make a part of a building look like a duck's bill or a pigeon wing and call it biomimicry, for example.

We can do much better. And we have done much better in the past. As a matter of fact, a living tradition can be regarded as the most profound biomimicry of all because of the fact that it doesn't just mimic the processes of one creature. Rather, it mimics the process of life itself by taking ideas and giving them a life of their own, so that they can persist for centuries or sometimes even millennia after their originators are dead and likely forgotten.

Great Variety in a Narrow Range: No two buildings are identical, but the places have strong character. You likely know where all these places are because of their character.

It isn't just the process of life that living traditions mimic; the products (buildings) also bear striking resemblances to natural things in this way: Within a given place, buildings created by a living tradition have great variety, but within a narrow range. No two people are exactly alike (except identical twins) but even though we're all different, nobody would mistake any of us for a wolf or an octopus.

Great variety gives a place life. A narrow range creates character. It's easy to get great variety in buildings by having no rules, but then there's no character, and it could be anywhere. It's also not hard to narrow the range to zero and mechanically duplicate the same thing over and over, but then there's no life, and people characterize the place as "cookie-cutter." New Urbanist places, as good as they are on other counts, often get charged with being "plastic" because they've worked so hard to get the houses right that they're all too much alike.

Putting great variety and a narrow range together is baffling. Without a living tradition, it's about as hard as trying to give life to a Frankenstein monster. But using the natural process of a living tradition, it simply becomes the natural thing to do. It's simply "this is how we build here."

HARMONY *with* NATURAL LAWS

Humans also resonate with natural laws, such as the law of gravity. In other words, they don't just expect for things to stand up, but also to *look like* they are capable of standing up. Nobody except an architect wants to walk into a building built so thinly that it appears to be in imminent danger of collapse.

INCORPORATION *of* NATURAL FORMS

Humanity's need to use natural forms in architecture is evident from the earliest dawn of conscious design that we're

Human & Plant Forms

aware of. Humans, other creatures, and plant forms have all been incorporated freely through the ages. The most important buildings were often the most liberally adorned with natural forms. Architecture of the past century largely discarded the use of natural forms, opting for a "machine aesthetic" instead. Most non-architects agree, however, that the banishment of natural forms from architecture normally leaves it colder, more sterile, and less lovable than that which came before.

HARMONY *with the* REGION

Much of this book deals with architecture appropriate to regional conditions, climate, and culture because it's more sensible. It turns out that it's more lovable, too, in a mysterious way: Let's say you're from Beaufort, South Carolina, and you travel to the Tuscany for a vacation. Let's also say that you're like countless other people who are completely charmed with Tuscan farmhouses, but your house in Beaufort looks like the one above. Although you are totally in love with Tuscan farmhouses in Tuscany, you'd probably also agree that they would look ridiculous built just down the street from your home in Beaufort. How can this be?

I believe that most people have a built-in sense of harmony that detects basic appropriateness of things. For example, this sense of harmony appears to be able to discern whether buildings have useful reasons for looking the way they do, or whether it's just some slathered-on style. Maybe regionally appropriate architecture isn't even consciously designed to be lovable, but is instead simply built to meet basic needs. But it seems like the more we sense connections between regional conditions that form it and the resulting architecture, the more we love it, even if we're from a far different place halfway around the world. How else can we explain why Tuscan farmhouses are great in Tuscany but silly in Beaufort?

STACKING *the* DECK

So what is the conclusion of this matter of lovable things? Many ask how it is possible to know what others love, and some are put off by the proposition that we might know what future generations may love. This suspicion is built on the notion that beauty is in the eye of the beholder, and is predicated upon the model of architecture as fashion. But architecture can do so much

better than that. Because that which is the most intensely of our time today is also the most quickly "outtadate" tomorrow.

So while it is not possible to guess what architectural fashions might be like in 20 or 30 human generations (or even next year, for that matter,) it most certainly is possible to stack the deck in our favor by building things that incorporate patterns that reflect timeless aspects of our humanity. Doing so extends the efficiency of the places and buildings we build today long into an uncertain future.

the DURABLE BUILDINGS

Our ancestors once built for the ages. Their buildings were durable enough to last for centuries, and because they were Lovable, they often did. Can we conceive of buildings that last for a millennium again? Durability is essential to sustainability. This should be considered so self-evident that it needs no explanation. Inexplicably, most so-called "sustainable" buildings today are still built of materials and in configurations that make it unlikely that they will even last a century. It cannot be sustained if it is not durable. This should be considered a self-evident truth. Let's study several ways we've missed that mark recently in order to understand how to hit it in the future:

Strength *vs.* Durability

Durability should not be confused with strength. Modern materials are typically stronger than the older, traditional materials they replace. Steel beams are many times stronger than wood beams. Reinforced concrete is substantially stronger than handmade brick. Steel wall panels are several times stronger than wood siding. But strength alone doesn't mean that any of these materials will last longer.

Steel melts in fires, whereas wood chars very slowly. I still remember a shocking picture I saw in architecture school, where a part new, part old building had burned and the nearly-melted steel beams were draped limply over a charred but still strong timber beam. When they rebuilt the building, they were able to shore up the charred timber beams, but the steel had to be removed entirely and scrapped. I wish I could find that picture again.

Reinforced concrete depends on embedded steel rebars for its strength. Because concrete is like a very dense sponge, water will eventually soak into it if it's exposed to the weather. When the rebar rusts and the encasing concrete pops off as a result, much of the strength is gone, as you can see in the bridge on the previous page.

NATURAL USES *of* MATERIALS

Just because it's a traditional material doesn't guarantee its durability, however. Brick used to build bearing walls like those on this building can last for centuries. The Pantheon in Rome is built primarily of brick, and it is nearly two thousand years old. But brick used unnaturally as a veneer can have a lifespan as short as a few decades. There are several reasons for this: While brick bearing walls are made of several layers, or "wythes" of brick, and therefore very sturdy, a brick veneer is only one wythe thick and is therefore subject to all sorts of movement. The middle of a big panel of brick veneer even moves slightly every time the wind blows.

Movement isn't the only problem with brick veneer. While it's possible to support brick over door or window openings with arches or with stone lintels, this job is far more frequently done with steel angles. Problem is, steel rusts. So in a century or less (much less if they're not properly maintained) the steel angles must be replaced.

The steel angle problem gets far worse when the brick veneer gets very tall. If a brick veneer wall is more than a couple stories tall, then the entire wall is supported on steel elements called "shelf angles" that run entirely around the building.

Shelf angles typically occur at every floor level. When the shelf angles rust out, replacing them is a mammoth and very expensive task that requires repair workers to remove small triangular-shaped sections of brick so that they can cut out and reinstall short sections of the shelf angle. That's what they had to do on this building. The cost of this sort of brick veneer repair can be so daunting that in some cases, it makes more financial sense to rip it all off and replace it with some sort of cheap metal cladding. Clearly, brick veneer is the poster child for the unsustainability of using traditional materials in an unnatural fashion.

the MAINTENANCE-FREE MYTH

There is another way that buildings can fail to achieve durability, and this one is the most nefarious of all, because its purveyors are selling the idea of durability while providing the exact opposite. This is something I call the Maintenance-Free Myth. We've all heard the sales pitch: install this stuff, and you'll never have to paint/patch/change the washers/whatever again. It's compelling, because who really likes doing a lot of household maintenance chores? Nobody I know.

The Maintenance-Free Myth is best illustrated by its poster child, which is vinyl siding. Let's say the salesmen got to you and you vinylized your Victorian, covering up all the wood siding with vinyl, and clapping vinyl panels all over your gingerbread and trimwork. Behind the vinyl, you may now be collecting moisture and deteriorating the woodwork so that when your kids or some other future resident decides to undo the damage you've done, they're likely to find a rotten mess when they remove the vinyl.

See the flames coming off the grill? See the vinyl siding? Guess what happens next?

But that's only half the story, because in a few years, some of the vinyl will fail. Maybe your puppy decides to teethe on a strip of siding low on the wall, or maybe you scoot the grill a bit too close and some of it melts. In any case, here's what happens next: You first try to replace it with extra siding you stored up over the garage for just such a time as this. But it's been protected for years, while the siding on the wall has been weathering, so there's no way it will match. So you have two choices: patch it, and endure a mismatched mess from now on, or do what most people do and rip it all off, cart it off to the landfill, and start over. The bottom line is this: when so-called "no maintenance" materials fail, they fail catastrophically so you have to replace every bit of the materials, not just the damaged piece.

NON-STANDARD COMPONENTS

There's another way that buildings can lack durability. Once, most building components were fairly similar. For example, if you needed to replace a window sash in 1920, pretty much any millwork shop in town could make it for you and it would work, because they all used the same knives to shape their components. Today, however, each window manufacturer makes their own proprietary components, so if you want to replace anything, you must go back to the same manufacturer (if they're still in business) and hope that they're still mak-

ing that model of window. If either of these things aren't true, then you've gotta rip the entire window out, re-frame the opening (because the old window likely won't match the standard size of the new one) and put in a whole new window.

HIGHLY PROCESSED MATERIALS

There's another aspect to this problem: Highly processed materials like alumi-

num require far more energy to create than less-processed materials like brick. Highly processed materials require more specialized production facilities, so they are likely to be created further from your building site, and hence must be shipped further. They are also less sustainable because like with the windows, when a component fails and if the system is no longer manufactured, then the entire system may have to be replaced. Use highly processed materials only in places where nothing processed less can do the job.

[229]

the FLEXIBLE BUILDINGS

Flexible Buildings are those that can be used for many uses over the centuries, long after the original need they were built for has passed from the present into memory. We cannot even conceive of how many uses a building might be put to in thirty or forty generations, which is how long buildings may last if they are both lovable and durable. So the interiors must be able to be recycled again and again for future uses that may not even exist today.

This means that the program of uses the architect uses to design the building may be one of the most over-rated things in architecture. If you design the best possible post office, then it could easily be torn down once a post office is no longer needed there. But if you design the best possible building instead, then it can be used for many things over the centuries, including as a post office.

How is it possible to prepare for things that we cannot anticipate? Here are the things we know, or at least the things we *think* we know:

PROXIMITY *to the* STREET

This may sound strange as the first item, but buildings become more flexible the closer they are located to the street. Looking at two extremes makes this obvious: Good Main Street buildings pull all the way up to the sidewalk, and they're used for more purposes than any other building in town. During prosperous times, they may have shops on the first two levels and offices above. In times of decline, they may have offices, residences, or even storage on the first level, but when the town's economy recovers, they may have shops below and apartments above again. At the other extreme, consider a building that's five miles off the street. It's good for only a very few things: either a very wealthy person's estate house, or an explosives factory that needs to be that far from town so nobody outside the factory is killed in the event of an accident.

SIMPLICITY *of* MASSING

The most flexible buildings are usually ones with a simple shape. A simple shape allows a building to be used for many

Mews are usually simple boxes. Many here are still used for residences, but the one in the front has been converted to a pub, and there's a grocery & deli further to the right.

things over the years. A complicated shape into which a particular use fits like a hand into a glove is much less likely to be useful for other purposes later on.

ATTACHMENT *to the* SHELL

The durable shell of Flexible Buildings should allow for attachment of interior improvements. Walls and cabinetry are two common components that need to be attached to the building shell, but they are by no means the only things that need hard attachments. Finishes are easier to manage, because they can

What Not to Do: Far too wiggly for most uses.

be adhered and then peeled off later. But the heavier things need solid attachment. Masonry allows this very easily, because anchors may be installed in any mortar joint. Concrete, on the other hand, isn't so easy because there's no natural point of attachment. When the wall, cabinet, or whatever is eventually removed, the point of attachment is a scar that requires skilful patching. Panelized walls made up of light components are a bigger challenge, because the panels often don't easily allow attachment at unexpected places, and everything about a future renovation is unexpected today. Least flexible of all is a glass curtain wall because the only possible places to

[233]

attach are to the mullions, and once you've done so, the screw holes are nearly impossible to patch when the wall is moved in the future.

PIPES *and* DUCTS

Because our history over the past two centuries has been one of increasing the number of pipes rather than decreasing them, flexible buildings should have a strategy for channeling services through all their rooms. In a former life, I ran a conventional architecture firm. Clients, on a number of occasions, used a building's inability to be easily air conditioned as an excuse for tearing it down.

CEILING HEIGHTS

Because our energy outlook over the next thousand years is most uncertain, buildings designed to be naturally frugal will also be more flexible. We'll look at frugality in detail in a moment, but one item bears noting here: Buildings with low ceilings in hot climates, for example, may not be considered flexible enough to save in the future, regardless of how frugal they are today. Ceiling height, therefore, should be determined by what makes the most sense for the regional climate.

Simplicity *of the* Circulation

Architects have recently had a strange love affair with building circulation. People might spend hours at a time in a room and only seconds at a time circulating between rooms, but architects often fixate on circulation. It begins in architecture school, where the first query from professors is often "tell me about your circulation." I've wondered at times if some architects might have "freeway envy"? Look at drawings of the early Modernist visionaries, and the buildings usually were set within a context of freeways with cars zipping everywhere.

Both vertical and horizontal circulation are often "expressed" today, which is architect-speak for putting it where you can see it. We've all seen the elevators rising up the side of a building in clean glass sheathes. Or maybe it's the ramps or escalators sliding along the side of the building. Stairs, too, often get popped out. As a matter of fact, some buildings have so much circulation sprouting all over their skins like some contagious infection that it's not immediately clear what sort of building is behind all that. And in any case, it's not good for the overall health of the building, which would be much better served if the circulation quietly did its job serving the rooms where we work and live.

the FRUGAL BUILDINGS

Frugal Buildings can be considered frugal in eight aspects: The first three are their frugality with the energy to construct and operate buildings, and the energy of transportation associated with the occupation of the buildings. Next are frugality of materials to construct, the recycling of the materials of construction and operation, and our stewardship of the water

Diagramming Frugality: Here's how the parts fit together

and the air that surrounds the buildings. Finally, frugality extends both to how we conserve the nature around us, and also how we conserve our own wellness.

Gizmo Green, as described in Part One's *2 ~ the Supply-Side Focus*, deals almost entirely with various aspects of frugality, but it's only a part of the story because there are many aspects of frugality that can be achieved in more natural ways, some of which have been proven for centuries. Specifics of these eight aspects of frugality are as follows:

[237]

ENERGY *of* CONSTRUCTION

Proponents of Gizmo Green profess their concern with energy required to construct buildings. But Gizmo Green was born from a fascination with all things technical. Its practitioners therefore prefer highly-processed high-tech materials over traditional materials. The problem is that traditional materials generally contain much less embodied energy per pound than the high-tech ones. So while Gizmo Green makes some contributions to reducing energy required to construct buildings by calling for materials extracted and regionally, living traditions do the same, and they also prefer materials that have been processed less, embodying less energy.

ENERGY *of* OPERATION

Energy required to operate buildings is the largest measuring-stick of Gizmo Green. Here, proponents of Gizmo Green have made large contributions. Unfortunately, those contributions focus heavily on the mechanical operation of the buildings, and because machines have a lifespan much less than a Durable building, they will eventually break down and need to be replaced. Our recent track record has been one of continually better machines, so it could be argued that eventual breakdown is actually a good thing since it requires the machine to be replaced with a more efficient machine. But buildings created from living traditions that condition space first by passive means are more certain to work for the life of the building because passive means are not dependent upon any particular technology.

Energy *of* Transportation

Reducing transportation energy by making places more compact is nowhere on the Gizmo Green radar screen. The New Urbanism, however, has been developing methods of producing places where people can walk to work, to shop, to school, and to play for decades. Transportation energy is an essential component of any serious conversation on true sustainability.

Construction Materials

Gizmo Green is rightly concerned with building from rapidly renewable materials or recycled materials. Living traditions did this for millennia out of necessity, because a tradition that lived long enough to be passed down for generations obviously could not be built with

materials that ran out in short order. The difference is that living traditions more easily use low-tech materials because they have no predisposition to aesthetics of high technology.

RECYCLING

Methods of recycling today have been almost completely defined by the proponents of Gizmo Green. Credit should be given where it is due. Re-use is the best policy, of course, but recycling is far better than throwing stuff away.

WATER *and* AIR

Gizmo Green is also highly concerned with our stewardship of the water and air around us, and rightfully so. There are two downsides. Within buildings, when mechanical systems which are the heart of Gizmo Green fail or are somehow compromised, then the entire building is likely to perform very poorly if at all until the parts arrive and the technician is able to install them. We have all likely experienced a mechanically-conditioned building rendered uninhabitable when its systems fail. The second downside is that Gizmo Green's near-religious regard for bodies of water does not allow urbanism near wa-

ter; all that is allowed is a working port. But great cities were often built along a manmade hard edge of a river, a lake, or an ocean. Think Paris, Rio, Venice, Hong Kong, or Chicago. This allows close contact between humans and the water, therefore making the city a more enticing place for people to live compactly, leaving more of nature untouched, which helps achieve this next item:

Protecting *the* Nature Around Us

Gizmo Green is rightfully concerned with stewardship of natural places, and addresses it in a number of ways, such as avoiding light pollution, recycling rather than consuming new materials, encouraging brownfield redevelopment, encouraging renewable energy, etc. The New Urbanism protects the environment by enticing people to live more compactly in order to leave more of nature untouched, and to pollute less by driving less. Living traditions have always been based on making do with the materials and craft sets that are available regionally, and doing things in the least invasive way.

HUMAN WELLNESS

The final aspect of Frugality is the conservation of our own wellness. Nearly everyone agrees that places and buildings contribute at least to wellness of the body. Most agree they can likely contribute to wellness of the mind. Some believe that buildings and places might possibly even contribute to wellness of the spirit. The last one is an article of faith you can consider on your own, but I'll say for the record that I firmly believe the first two are true.

Gizmo Green addresses primarily chemical aspects of wellness, such as the use of low-VOC building materials and proper ventilation to remove indoor pollutants. The New Urbanism addresses physical wellness by encouraging walking, and also wellness of mind by allowing for the creation of community rather than just the warehousing of residents. Living traditions fulfill a broad range of wellness roles too comprehensive to list here that can best be encapsulated within the notion of engaging each person in a living process of achieving a sustainable way of life for them and their world.

Frugality Report Card: Who's carrying the load in each of the elements of frugality.

The Frugality Report Card illustrates what I've been saying for several pages: Gizmo Green makes clear contributions to most of the elements of frugality, but with the exception of recycling, Gizmo Green is not the sole contributor.

Unfortunately, most of the green building discussions heard today on the biggest stages still deal only with Gizmo Green solutions. Even the term "green building" shows its incompleteness by dealing only with buildings and implicitly excluding places. Let's be highly explicit here: Gizmo Green measures are usually smart and normally helpful. But, by themselves, they are incomplete.

*Here's the full Original Green Report Card as conditions
stand as this book is being written in the late winter of 2010.*

The full Original Green Report Card shows just how small a part Gizmo Green fills in the full picture of real sustainability. It also shows how many gaps there are in some of the other foundations. Clearly, the challenges before us will test our ingenuity and try our resolve. Let's put every resource we have to work, especially those which have been proven to work for nearly all of human history. *Why not use tools that work?*

[244]

Part Four

What Can I Do?

The Top 10 Things You Can Do to Be Green

The things we've talked about so far are really big things. In a highly populated region, an Original Green living tradition might involve millions of people. You might say "Just thinking about trying to get all those people to do anything makes my head hurt! And it could take years to do some of these things! What can I start doing right now?" These are the top ten things you can do as part of your everyday sustainable life.

I should warn you that, as you get closer to Item #1, it's going to sound harder and harder, because these are the things that make a more serious difference, but the serious difference they will make in your life will be worth it in many ways. For example, I made a major change in my life almost seven years ago that took me to a highly walkable place. I expected to spend a lot less on gas... and I do. But there were side-effects I didn't expect. For example, I lost 60 pounds because of all the walking, transforming me from a tired old man at age 43 to a far more healthy and energetic person today. So here are the top ten; if they begin to sound impossibly hard as you approach #1, then just remember that they just might be impossibly good instead:

10 ~ Do All *of the* Stuff You Already Know

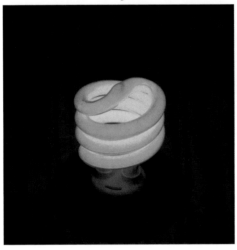

Change your light bulbs. Change the filter in your furnace. Install a programmable thermostat. Buy Energy Star appliances. Insulate your water heater. Air-dry your clothes instead of putting them in an electric dryer. Turn off things you're not using. Buy fresh food instead of frozen food. Avoid heavily packaged products. Keep your tires aired up. Wear a sweater in the winter, and dress lightly in summertime. And by all means, recycle!

These are all great things to do... no doubt about it. But they don't solve the problem of living sustainably today. Instead, they make our extremely wasteful modern lifestyles just a little bit less wasteful. So remember: these things are good, but they're not the game-changers. Make sure you *do them*, but don't *stop with them* and think you're living sustainably. Living truly sustainably requires bigger changes.

9 ~ Give *a* Gift *to the* Street

 Make sure to give a gift to the street where you live and where you work. A gift to the street is something that either refreshes people (like a sidewalk cafe), shelters them (like an awning over the sidewalk), delights them (like the frontage garden shown here), directs them (like a tower to walk toward), entertains them (like an interesting storefront), informs them (like a clock or sundial), helps them remember (like a memorial), or gives them a place to rest. There is no act so neighborly as doing something kind for someone you might not even know.

"Sounds nice," you might ask, "but why does a gift to the street make the top ten list?" Here's why: Few things we do have a bigger impact than people getting outside and walking, for reasons we've talked about throughout this book. If the homes and the shops in your town each gave a gift to the street, think how much more interesting it would be to walk there! And this is the easiest one... depending on your gift, it's something you might even be able to do today.

8 ~ CHOOSE IT *for* LONGER *than* YOU'LL USE IT

We're consumers... we've been told this almost since birth. Consumers use things for awhile, and then throw them away. Some things last long enough to sell, but our consumer mindset shows through:

"I won't own this house for more than 7-10 years," the standard story goes, "... so why should I care what it's like in 50 or 100 years?" This incredibly short-term attitude has burdened us with a world where every generation must buy a new house, because the ones we built 40 years ago (or less) are falling apart. This weight we've been saddled with is responsible in many ways for the current economic crisis, and is the very definition of unsustainability. It's time to unburden ourselves and our children, and those that come after them. Living sustainably requires things that endure, and can be passed down as things of value to another generation.

7 ~ Choose Smaller Stuff *with* Double Duty

Americans have taken the notion of single-duty to an ugly extreme known as "redundancy." Instead of having one thing that does several jobs, we have several things that each do the same job, just in case we get bored with one of them!

Our ancestors built flexible buildings such as homes with keeping rooms where most of the housekeeping was done, including eating. Today, we must have a dining room, an eat-in kitchen, a breakfast nook, and on it goes...just for eating!

American homes averaged about 1,100 square feet and housed about 4-1/2 people just after World War II. Today, they've bloated to over twice that size, but contain families only half as large. That means there's nearly four times as much conditioned space per person! And even so, we have so much stuff that won't fit in our bloated houses that we've made the mini-storage industry a $17 *billion* per year business... bigger than the movie industry! Having rooms and choosing things that can do more than just one job won't completely solve our problems, but it'll certainly be a start in the right direction.

6 ~ LIVE WHERE FRIENDS VISIT UNANNOUNCED

The best places, such as these historic neighborhoods in Charleston, don't require your friends to check in with a guard before coming to see you. Gated "communities" have huge sustainability problems. They aren't really communities, of course, because they don't contain all the parts of a real community, like shops selling the basic necessities of life on Main Street, schools, and offices. They just contain houses... and maybe a few recreational "amenities." As a result, residents of gated subdivisions must drive everywhere. So even if the houses have a low carbon footprint, the environmental costs of living there are high.

Gated subdivisions also fail in their stated objective of building secure places because by segregating society, life gets more dangerous outside the gates than it would have been otherwise... and you can't stay inside forever. The safest and most valuable places have always been real communities with large, medium, and small houses in each neighborhood. These are places, as we've seen, where you might live just a few blocks from some of the firefighters and police that protect you, the waiter who serves your lunch, or the barista who makes your espresso in the morning. And the new neighbor around the corner on the rear lane just might be your kid who just graduated from college!

5 ~ Operate Naturally

We've come to depend on machines in almost every facet of our lives, including in every room of the buildings that we build. Machines doubtlessly make our lives easier, but do they always make them better? Think of the most memorable moments of your life... how many of the memories etched most indelibly into your mind came as a result of something you were doing with a machine?

Now think about how many of the memories included a scent on a breeze through the open window or the angle of an early morning sunbeam. Delight is often a side-effect of buildings that operate naturally for most of the year. The most noticeable effect of conditioning buildings entirely with machines is a big utility bill. So build a naturally frugal home or shop instead, and cut the equipment off for months at a time.

4 ~ RAISE *a* VICTORY GARDEN

Much of the food we eat today, as we've discussed, needs a passport to get to our table and must be genetically engineered to endure that long journey, leaving it less nourishing and not tasting nearly so good as food grown nearby. Taste for yourself: All you need is a grocery store apple and a local heritage apple.

You can avoid all the problems, risks, and costs of industrially grown food simply by raising a victory garden in your yard. Not only will you know exactly what has gone into your food, but you won't need to burn a drop of gas to get the food to your table! You'll be surprised at how much of your food you can raise at home, and will be doing your part to help create a nourishing place. You don't need a huge yard for your garden, either. It can be as small as a terrace garden or even a window garden. You can also start or join a community garden or a Community Supported Agriculture (CSA) group.

3 ~ Build Garden Rooms *in* Your Yard

Grass lawns must be mowed at least weekly, burning fuel. And it's tempting to clean the lawn between mowings with a leaf blower, but leaf blowers generate stunning amounts of greenhouse gases. But those reasons are overshadowed by the benefits of garden rooms.

Build a dinner garden, a breakfast terrace, a hearth garden, a kitchen garden, and maybe a master garden. The dinner garden is where you eat your big outdoor meals. The breakfast terrace is nearer the kitchen, and is for quick meals. The hearth garden may contain an outdoor fireplace, and is your outdoor living room. The kitchen garden is the center of your Victory Garden, although parts of the landscape in other garden rooms can be edible, too. The master garden is accessible only from the master suite, and is the couple's private realm.

Make sure that you furnish each garden room, so you can sit and spend time in each of them. You likely won't believe this until you actually try it, but when you spend more time outdoors, then you get acclimated to your local climate in all but the most extreme times of year. When you do, then you'll need less full-body refrigeration (or heating) when you return indoors... so for much of the year, you might be able to just open the windows rather than hitting the thermostat. And because much of your living space is outdoors, you'll need less conditioned space indoors... which you're conditioning less. No single measure does more to make a home frugal.

2 ~ LIVE WHERE YOU CAN WALK *to the* GROCERY

If you can walk to the grocery, you don't need something the size of an SUV to stock up on two weeks' worth of rations at the Super-Center. Instead, you can simply decide what you'd like for dinner this evening, and then carry it home. You'll get some exercise on a pleasant walk, and your food will be much fresher. But this is much more important than just groceries.

If you can walk for groceries, then you likely live where you can walk to many other necessities of life, too. This means that you likely can drive a lot less than the 10 car trips per day that most Americans average. This only works when your neighborhood gives you a choice of ways to get around, especially encouraging walking and biking.

1 ~ Make *a* Living Where You're Living

The most important thing you can do yourself is to do what all our ancestors once did... make a living where you're living. If you were a fisherman, for example, then you lived in a fishing village like this one. Unfortunately, it has been illegal to live where you work for much of the last century. In the 20th century, zoning separated everything into pods, and you were forced to drive everywhere.

Fortunately, the New Urbanists have been working for thirty years to change all that. New codes like the SmartCode are now replacing antiquated zoning laws that segregated everything. So if your city or town is working to implement a SmartCode, please give it your full support. If not, the internet is also making it possible to work from home, or to work out of a branch office in your neighborhood center rather than commuting to the city center. So while this sounds at first like a tough thing to do, you may find that it's not only possible, but you may also find it to be one of the most liberating things you've ever done. Think about it. Yes, it's likely a big change... but it may be one of the best changes you've ever made.

FINAL WORDS

Look at the image below. One side of each of these hills is teeming with life; the other is nearly barren. The difference between life and no life is just a slight tipping of the hillside. You can do the ten preceding things yourself, but we need living traditions to get the bigger things in this book done.

Maybe the idea of starting a new living tradition seems like far too daunting a task; many architects and planners even believe that living traditions are impossible today, so why try? But living traditions are the only proven means of delivering Original Green wisdom to everyone, so we really must do everything we can to bring them to life in our day.

So what can you do to help? You never know for sure until you try, but chances are good that in some part of what you do for passion, or what you do for a living, you just might be able to play a part in tipping the balance from no life to life in the place where you live. We need you!

~Steve Mouzon, January 30, 2010

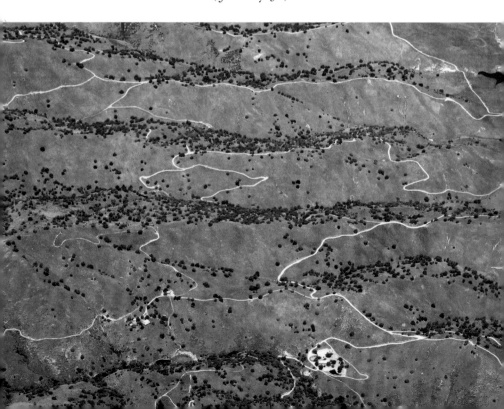

Resources

The following pages contain a number of resources to assist in your work to help establish an Original Green living tradition where you live. Please contact me via email if you know of resources that should be included in future editions. The address is: ideas@mouzon.com. I can't guarantee a response to every email, but I can guarantee that every one will be read.

ORIGINAL GREEN WEBSITE
WWW.ORIGINALGREEN.ORG

The Original Green website is a growing collection of Original Green resources. Please revisit it regularly, as things are being added frequently.

ORIGINAL GREEN BLOG
WWW.ORIGINALGREEN.ORG/OG/BLOG/BLOG.HTML

I post to the Original Green Blog regularly. It's intended to be incisive and provocative. Please join the conversation; all comments are welcome! This book was significantly improved as a result of comments on this blog.

ORIGINAL GREEN TWITTER TIMELINE
@STEVEMOUZON (TWITTER.COM/STEVEMOUZON)

I Twitter about many issues surrounding the Original Green and living traditions. Often, I'll post fragments of ideas as I'm developing them, hoping that others join the conversation. Many of the ideas in this book have been refined as a result of Twitter conversations.

ORIGINAL GREEN FACEBOOK CAUSE
APPS.FACEBOOK.COM/CAUSES/154766

Please join the Original Green cause on Facebook. There are over 10,000 members all over the world as I'm writing this.

ORIGINAL GREEN BOOK IMAGES
SAMOUZON.ZENFOLIO.COM

If you like the images in this book, many of them are available on this site. Most are $3.99 each for high-res jpg files.

Original Green News Releases
www.originalgreen.org/OG/Subscribe.html

I occasionally do mailings on items I believe could be important to those interested in the Original Green.

Useful Stuff Blog
usefulstuff.posterous.com

The Useful Stuff blog is like a second brain for me, because whenever I figure something out, I'll post it there so I can remember it later on. Some of the items posted deal with sustainability issues, while others vary as widely as drawing systems, travel tips, and social media techniques.

New Urban Guild Website
www.newurbanguild.com

The New Urban Guild is a remarkable group of several dozen architects, designers, and urbanists dedicated to the creation of increasingly sustainable places and buildings. I founded the Guild in 2001.

Guild Foundation Website
www.guildfoundation.org

The Guild Foundation is a 501(c)3 non-profit created by the Guild to research sustainable place-making, and to provide education and resources based on what was learned. It hosts the Original Green initiative. If you're so inclined, this is where you can financially assist the Original Green.

Mouzon Design
www.mouzon.com

This is the design firm that Wanda and I operate.

LINKS

ORGANIZATIONS

Building Green: www.buildinggreen.com
Center for Applied Transect Studies: www.transect.org
Congress for the New Urbanism: www.cnu.org
Council for European Urbanism: www.ceunet.org
Institute of Classical Architecture/Classical America:
www.classicist.org
International Network for Traditional Building, Architecture
& Urbanism: www.intbau.org
Katrina Cottages: www.katrinacottages.com
Light Imprint: www.lightimprint.org
NextGen: www.cnunextgen.org
Pattern Language: www.patternlanguage.com
Prince's Foundation: www.princes-foundation.org
SmartCode: www.smartcodecentral.com
US Green Building Council: www.usgbc.org

SCHOOLS OF ARCHITECTURE

Andrews University: www.andrews.edu/arch
University of Miami: www.arc.miami.edu
Notre Dame: architecture.nd.edu

COMPANIES

Duany Plater-Zyberk & Company: www.dpz.com
Farr Associates: www.farrside.com
PlaceMakers: www.placemakers.com

BLOGS

Building Green: www.buildinggreen.com/live/rss.cfm
Civitas: traditional-building.com/clem_labine
CNU: www.cnu.org/blog/feed
Grist: feeds.grist.org/rss/kingdom/living-green
Jim Kunstler: feeds2.feedburner.com/clusterfucknation
Kaid Benfield: rss.nrdcfeeds.org/switchboard_kbenfield
New Urbanism Blog: newurbanismblog.com
Oil Drum: feeds.feedburner.com/theoildrum
Place Economics: www.placeeconomics.com/blog.html
PlaceShakers & NewsMakers: placeshakers.wordpress.com
Planetizen: www.planetizen.com/blog/feed
Slow Food: www.slowfoodusa.org/index.php/site
Steven Semes: traditional-building.com/Steve_Semes
Streetsblog: www.streetsblog.org/feed
Treehugger: feeds.feedburner.com/treehuggersite

ORIGINAL GREEN APP

Several of the blog feeds above can be found on the Original Green App, which is available from the iTunes App Store: http://bit.ly/6JP1On

BIBLIOGRAPHY

$20 Per Gallon, Christopher Steiner, Grand Central Publishing, 2009.

American Vitruvius: An Architects' Handbook of Civic Art, Werner Hegemann, Elbert Peets, Princeton Architectural Press, 1988.

Architecture: Choice or Fate, Léon Krier, Andreas Papadakis Publisher, 1998.

Architecture of Community, The, Léon Krier, Island Press, 2009.

Biomimicry, Janine M. Benyus, Harper Perennial, 2002.

Blink, Malcolm Gladwell, Little, Brown, and Company, 2005.

Boulevard Book, The, Allan Jacobs, Elizabeth Macdonald, Yodan Rofe, MIT Press, 2002.

Break Through, Michael Shellenberger & Ted Nordhaus, Houghton Mifflin, 2007.

Buildings of Main Street, The, Richard Longstreth, American Association for State & Local History Book Series, 2000.

Charter of the New Urbanism, Congress for the New Urbanism, McGraw-Hill, 2000.

Classical Architecture, Robert Adam, Harry N. Abrams, 1990.

Classical Orders of Architecture, The, Robert Chitham, Rizzoli, 1995.

Cradle to Cradle, William McDonough, Michael Braungart, North Point Press, 2002.

Death and Life of Great American Cities, The, Jane Jacobs, Vintage, 1992.

Elements of Style, The, Stephen Calloway, Simon & Schuster, 1996.

Field Guide to American Architecture, A, Carole Rifkind, Bonanza Books, 1980.

Free Agent Nation, Daniel H. Pink, Business Plus, 2002.

Geography of Nowhere, The, James Howard Kunstler, Simon & Schuster, 1993.

History of Architecture, A, Sir Banister Fletcher, Scribners, 1975.

Hot, Flat, and Crowded, Thomas L. Friedman, Farrar, Straus and Giroux, 2008.

In Defense of Food, Michael Pollan, Penguin, 2009.

Leadership and the New Science, Margaret J. Wheatley, Berrett Koehler Publishers, 2006.

Linked, Albert-Lazlo Barabasi, Plume, 2003.

Long Emergency, The, James Howard Kunstler, Atlantic Monthly Press, 2005.

Long Tail, The, Chris Anderson, Hyperion, 2008.

Made to Stick, Chip Heath & Dan Heath, Random House, 2007.

New Civic Art, The, Andres Duany, Elizabeth Plater-Zyberk, and Robert Alminana, Rizzoli, 2003.

New Rules for the New Economy, Kevin Kelly, Penguin, 1998.

New Urbanism: Best Practices Guide, Robert Steuteville, Philip Langdon, New Urban News Publications, 2009.

New Urbanism, The, Toward an Architecture of Community, Peter Katz, McGraw-Hill, 1994.

Omnivore's Dilemma, Michael Pollan, Penguin, 2007.

Outliers, Malcolm Gladwell, Little, Brown, 2008.

Parallel of the Classical Orders of Architecture, Johann Matthaus von Mauch, Acanthus Press, 1998.

Pattern Language, A, Christopher Alexander, Oxford University Press, 1977.

Place Making: Developing Town Centers, Main Streets, and Urban Villages, Charles Bohl, Urban Land Institute, 2002.

Rise of the Creative Class, The, Richard Florida, Basic Books, 2002.

Smart Growth Manual, The, Andrés Duany, Jeff Speck, Mike Lydon, McGraw-Hill, 2009.

Suburban Nation, Andrés Duany, Elizabeth Plater-Zyberk, Jeff Speck, North Point Press, 2001.

Timeless Way of Building, The, Christopher Alexander, Oxford University Press, 1979.

Tipping Point, The, Malcolm Gladwell, Back Bay Books, 2002.

Town Planning in Practice, Raymond Unwin, Princeton Architectural Press, 1994.

Tribes, Seth Godin, Portfolio Hardcover, 2008.

Twitter Power, Joel Comm, Wiley, 2009.

Unleashing the Ideavirus, Seth Godin, Hyperion, 2001.

Vision of Britain: A Personal View of Architecture, A, His Royal Highness The Prince of Wales, A. G. Carrick Ltd., 1989.

Whole New Mind, A, Daniel Pink, Riverhead Books, 2005.

Wikinomics: How Mass Collaboration Changes Everything, Don Tapscott & Anthony D. Williams, Portfolio Hardcover, 2008.

Wisdom of Crowds, The, James Surowiecki, Anchor, 2005.

World is Flat, The, Thomas L. Friedman, Picador, 2007.

GLOSSARY

This glossary includes terms to which I have assigned proper names in this book. It generally does not include proper names that are in common usage, such as Modernism, although it does contain some that others have coined such as New Urbanism because their usage is not so common. I assign proper names because they help important ideas to spread on their own, without the originator of the idea needing to be there to tell the story.

ACCESSIBLE PLACES

Places which you can access through a variety of means, not just by car; self-propelled (pedestrian and bicycle) access is required; others are highly encouraged.

AUTOMOTIVE POVERTY

Two components are: reduction of disposable income from $7,000 to $10,000 per year for each car a household must own in order to function, and reduction of available time due to Compulsory Commuting.

CLASSICAL-VERNACULAR SPECTRUM

System of arranging architectural patterns from the most organic to the most refined.

COMPULSORY COMMUTING

Condition created by places that discourage you from making a living where you're living.

CONSERVING ECONOMY

Economic model that existed for almost all of human history, where things are valued by how long they last.

Consuming Economy

Our current economic model, where economic health is measured by how much more we consume this year than last.

Durable Buildings

Buildings designed to have a durable shell, even if the interiors are designed to be recycled repeatedly over time.

Embodied Miles

Average distance traveled by all components of a product, from resource extraction to its place of use.

Everything Bubble

Our current state of affairs, where many measures of human life on earth, from population to species extinctions, are exhibiting bubble behavior.

Fifth Realm (Continental Patterns)

Those patterns of buildings or places found across a continent or shared by more than one continent, but not universal.

First Realm (Personal Patterns)

Those patterns of buildings or places found in the work of one designer or builder.

Flexible Buildings

Buildings designed to be adaptable to other uses in the future, including uses that do not currently exist.

FOURTH REALM (NATIONAL PATTERNS)

Those patterns of buildings or places found throughout a nation.

FRUGAL BUILDINGS

Buildings that use the energy of construction, materials of construction, energy of operation, materials of operation, and transportation associated with construction and operation in a frugal manner, and that are good stewards of the air and water around the buildings, the nature around the buildings, and our own wellness.

GIZMO GREEN

Sustainability ideas and methods which are primarily limited to better equipment and better materials.

GREAT DECLINE

The period from approximately 1925 to 1945; it included both a loss of generalists and a loss of sustainability.

INSANITY PRINCIPLE

The belief that one can keep doing what they've been doing but somehow get different results.

INVERSE INSANITY PRINCIPLE

The belief that one can do things in a dramatically different way from what they've been doing, but somehow get the same results.

KATRINA COTTAGE

Emergency housing solution developed in the wake of Hurricane Katrina based on the idea that emergency housing should be appropriate to regional conditions, climate, and culture, should be deliverable in all common construction methods, and should be of excellent design.

K<small>ERNEL</small> C<small>OTTAGE</small>

Cottage designed to grow unusually easily.

L<small>IVING</small> T<small>RADITION</small>

A tradition that, similar to a living spoken language, is in regular use by all the citizens of the region in which it is found. Operating system of the Original Green.

L<small>OST</small> G<small>ENERATION</small>

Second generation of Modernist architects.

L<small>OVABLE</small> B<small>UILDINGS</small>

Buildings designed to be loved by focusing on timeless principles humans have always been known to appreciate rather than the latest architectural fashions.

M<small>AINTENANCE</small>-F<small>REE</small> M<small>YTH</small>

Erroneous but widely-promoted belief that some materials do not require maintenance.

M<small>OST</small>-L<small>OVED</small> P<small>LACES</small>

Those places around the world that have been loved the longest and are usually valued the highest; Most-Loved Places pass the Tourist Test.

N<small>EW</small> U<small>RBANISM</small>

A set of principles for building places made up of neighborhoods that are compact, diverse, and walkable.

NEW URBANIST

A person who promotes and/or practices the principles of the New Urbanism.

NEXT-GENERATION HOUSING

Homes that are affordable to recent college graduates.

NEXT-GENERATION NEIGHBORHOODS

Neighborhoods that include a proportion of Next-Generation Housing that is similar to the proportion of people in the area that earn entry-level wages.

NEW TRADITIONALIST

A person engaged in the rebirth of traditions in architecture, the arts, or crafts.

NOURISHABLE PLACES

Places where, now or in the future, you could look out onto the fields or onto the waters from which a significant portion of your food comes.

NOVELTY PARADOX

How can we, at the same time, keep something going for centuries and also adapt to new conditions?

ORIGINAL GREEN

System of aggregating and distributing the wisdom of sustainability in order to create sustainable place (which are Nourishable, Accessible, Serviceable, and Securable) in which sustainable buildings (which are Lovable, Durable, Flexible, and Frugal) may be built.

Pedestrian Propulsion

The ability of streets to propel pedestrians along their way by enticing them to walk further. Better streets have stronger Pedestrian Propulsion.

Project:SmartDwelling

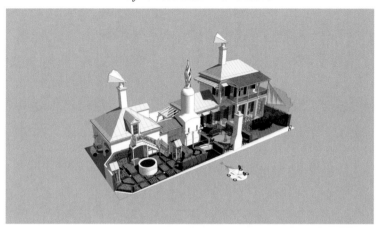

The New Urban Guild hosts the Project:SmartDwelling initiative, which is based on Original Green principles. For information on Project:SmartDwelling: http://bit.ly/4mD2Z1

SmartDwelling I, pictured above, was featured in the Wall Street Journal's Green House of the Future story on April 27, 2009. For links to the story and coverage it spawned, check this story on the Original Green Blog: bit.ly/rh4io

There have been numerous other SmartDwelling I posts on the Original Green Blog: www.originalgreen.org/OG/Blog/Blog.html. They're easy to spot; all of them contain "SmartDwelling I" somewhere in the title.

Second Realm (Local Patterns)

Those patterns of buildings or places found in a single locality.

SECURABLE PLACES

Places designed so that they can be made more secure if conditions warrant at some point in the future.

SERVICEABLE PLACES

Places where you can walk to your daily necessities within or adjacent to your own neighborhood; also, where those serving you those services can afford to live.

SINGLE-CREW WORKPLACE

Workplace of an ideal size to be run by a single crew.

SIXTH REALM (UNIVERSAL PATTERNS)

Those patterns of buildings or places found around the world.

SMALLER & SMARTER

Strategy of building smaller buildings that live large, so as to accommodate people who would otherwise need larger buildings.

SMARTCODE

Revolutionary zoning code that makes places that are compact, mixed-use, and walkable; adopted instead of today's conventional zoning ordinances, which mandate unsustainable sprawl. (www.smartcodecentral.org)

THERMOSTAT AGE

The era that began with the invention mechanical heating, which allowed people to condition their buildings with the touch of a button.

THIRD REALM (REGIONAL PATTERNS)

Those patterns of buildings or places found throughout a region.

Tourist Test

Is a place good enough that people come from far away to visit it for the delight of being there, rather than to visit friends or to be entertained? If so, then may be one of the Most-Loved Places.

Transect

System of environmental management; extends from wilderness to the urban core, with different settings for each zone. (www.transect.org)

Transmission Device (*of* Living Traditions)

"We do this because..."

Wall of Terminal Weirdness

The point in the future when architecture cannot get any stranger. It will be brought on by the architectural profession's self-imposed necessity of uniqueness.

INSTITUTE OF
CLASSICAL ARCHITECTURE
& CLASSICAL AMERICA

OTHER TITLES *from the* CLASSICAL AMERICA SERIES *in* ART & ARCHITECTURE

The Golden City, Henry Hope Reed
The American Vignola, William R. Ware
The Architecture of Humanism, Geoffrey Scott
The Decoration of Houses, Edith Wharton and Ogden Codman, Jr.
Italian Villas and Their Gardens, Edith Wharton
The Classic Point of View, Kenyon Cox
What is Painting?, Kenyon Cox
Man as Hero: The Human Figure in Western Art, Pierce Rice
Greek and Roman Architecture in Classic Drawings, Hector d'Espouy
Monumental Classic Architecture in Great Britain and Ireland, Albert Richardson
Monograph of the Work of McKim, Mead & White, 1879-1915, Student Edition
The Library of Congress: Its Architecture and Decoration, Herbert Small
Letarouilly on Renaissance Rome, John Barrington Bayley
The New York Public Library: Its Architecture and Decoration, Henry Hope Reed
The Elements of Classical Architecture, George Gromort
Palaces of the Sun King: Versailles, Trianon, Marly, the Chateaux of Louis XIV, Berndt Dams and Andrew Zega
Bricks and Brownstone: The New York Row House 1783-1929, Charles Lockwood

The Architecture of the Classical Interior, Steven W. Semes
Classical Architecture for the Twenty-First Century: An Introduction to Design, J. François Gabriel
The United States Capitol: Its Architecture and Decoration, Henry Hope Reed
Arthur Brown Jr.: Progressive Classicist, Jeffrey T. Tillman
Classical Swedish Architecture and Interiors 1650-1840, Johan Cederlund
*Carolands: Ernest Sanson, Achille Duchene, Willis Polk, Michael Middleton Dwyer; produced by Charles Davey
The Theory of Mouldings, C. Howard Walker and Richard Sammons
Building Details, Frank M. Snyder
Antiquities of Athens, James Stuart and Nicholas Revett
Get Your House Right, Architectural Elements to Use & Avoid, Marianne Cusato & Ben Pentreath with Richard Sammons and Leon Krier
The Study of Architectural Design, John F. Harbeson, John Blatteau, and Sandra L. Tatman
Edwin Howland Blashfield: Master American Muralist, Mina Wiener, editor
The Vatican and Saint Peter's Basilica of Rome, Paul M. Letarouilly
The Future of the Past, Steven W. Semes

[280]